Master Cricut Design Space

I0481243

An Essential Guide To Learn Everything About

Cricut Machine and Design Space + Amazing

Projects Ideas Along With Guidelines

KAYLA PIERCE

will any legal responsibility or blame be held against the publisher for any reparation, damages, or monetary loss due to the information herein, either directly or indirectly.

Respective authors own all copyrights not held by the publisher.

The information herein is offered for informational purposes solely and is universal as so. The presentation of the information is without a contract or any type of guarantee assurance.

The trademarks that are used are without any consent, and the publication of the trademark is without permission or backing by the trademark owner. All trademarks and brands within this book are for clarifying purposes only and are owned by the owners themselves, not affiliated with this document.

Table of Contents

Introduction

Welcome to the Cricut world. You might have your machine and now you possibly think, "What now?" You might even be too scared to pull it out of the package. Don't be scared, this is why this book is here. It is supposed to be a brilliant thing to use and the options are limitless as far as it is an excellent machine that you can do with! You should do exactly that! Being a crafter, there are several options for you and the applications of a Cricut are infinite. Whether you're a scrapbooker or a successful business owner, there are loads of choices for using the Cricut. It's a perfect way to be a skilled crafter and find a device or partner that allows you the opportunity and pursue your passion. Happily, Cricut has created an awesome tool with advanced cutting technologies for everyone who wants to go in crafts that will aid you cut, build, and carry all the beautiful art ideas of yours to life.

Knowing what devices and accessories that can be used with the Cricut to minimize your time for preparation and save you headaches. The Cricut is versatile is and can be utilized to connect at any point in the project with several forms of materials. This book is for beginners and contains advanced Cricut projects as well, where you can discover everything you need to know about what the Cricut machine and how to bring the best out of this device. We will show all the confidential information that will enable you to use your device in no time like a specialist!

Chapter No. 1 Cricut Basics

The best thing about Cricut is that projects are endless. You might decide to have your wall lettering, or you might choose to make a nursery at home, and you would need to make that distinct wall painting with several letters. Instead of spending several hours cutting with blades and carving with knives or any other cutting device, you just need a Cricut machine. You do not even need to hire someone for hand painting because you can do that yourself. People are happy that you are not exposed to this knowledge so that they can make some cash from you. The die-cut machine produces those precise cuts which children and other professional needs. There are several die-cut stickers you can get from this machine. This machine also allows you to render wedding favors and party favors quickly by helping in the creating process of tags, bags, boxes, and several other party creations. These pieces can come in several forms like gift bags, banners, hats, etc. These and many more can fit the theme of any party because you are making them. As much as someone would love to shy away from the scrapbook stuff one just cannot. Now, just picture your daughter or your son getting married and you present him/her with a scrapbook having pictures from the very first day they stepped into this planet to where they are now. Gifts like this sound odd, but they are invaluable because you are not giving out a utensil or a tool you are giving out those memories. Scrapbooks carry out many memories and those feelings you cannot give through your regular gifts.

If you have a Cricut machine and you have not gotten these supplies, we advise that you get them as soon as possible. We are aware that these supplies are grouped into different categories. First is the paper category which includes; adhesive cardstock, cereal box, copy paper, flocked paper, cardboard paper, notebook paper, flocked cardstock, foil embossed paper, freezer paper, glitter paper, kraft paper, kraft board, metallic paper, metallic poster board, photographs, photo framing mat, poster board, rice paper, wax paper, solid core cardstock, white core cardstock, photo framing mat, watercolor paper, freezer paper, foil poster board, etc.

We should not forget that the vinyl is another material that you need to make your work on the Cricut machine smooth. The Cricut machine can work on those delicate materials which can be used to make decals, stencils, graphics, and those beautiful signs too. You can cut through the following vinyl materials, chalkboard vinyl, dry erase vinyl, holographic vinyl, stencil vinyl, printable vinyl, matte vinyl, adhesive vinyl, printable vinyl, and glossy vinyl also. Furthermore, you may have so much experience in the fabric and textile world, and you want to infuse the Cricut machine. Some of the materials or fabrics that you can work with are; canvas, denim, cotton fabric, linen, leather, flannel, burlap, duck cloth, felt, metallic leather, polyester, printable materials, silk, wool felt and many more others. If you have not got your iron-on vinyl. Which is meant to be the heat transfer vinyl. You make use of this vinyl to decorate a t-shirt, tote bags, and other kinds of fabric items that you can think of like; printable iron-on, glitter iron-on, glossy iron-on, flocked iron-on, holographic sparkle iron-on, metallic iron-on, neon iron-on, foil iron-on, etc.

We should not narrow our minds to the materials mentioned above because there are several other materials which the Cricut can cut through or even work on some of them include; adhesive wood, corkboard, balsa wood, craft foam, aluminum sheets, corrugated paper, embossable foil, foil acetate, paint chips, plastic packaging, metallic vellum, printable sticker paper, stencil material, shrink plastic, wrapping paper, window cling, wood veneer, washi tape, birchwood, wrapping paper, wood veneer, plastic packaging, soda can, glitter foam, printable magnet sheets, etc. The Cricut maker can work on materials that are up to 2.4mm thick and other unique materials and distinctive fabrics like the; jersey, cashmere, chiffon, terry cloth, tweed, velvet, jute, knits, moleskin, fleece, and several others.

This machine can be found anywhere and everywhere. You can see these machines in schools, offices, craft shops, etc. You can make use of this Cricut machine for a school project, card stock projects as well as iron-on projects too. Making use of this machine to cut out window clings is not a bad idea at all. It is not limited to this because you also engage in projects that have to do with adhesive stencil and stencil vinyl also. You would remove the stencil vinyl after it is dried. This would leave a distinct imprint. You can also make use of this machine to create lovely fashion accessories like several pieces of jewelry. The Cricut machine allows you to make use of the faux leather for exceptional designs. Preschoolers and their instructors can benefit from this machine. Furthermore, you can print out photos or images from your computer while making use of this machine, especially from the printable magnets to those sticker papers, customized gifts, bags, etc.

Defining objects requires you to use other similar purposes to drive home your point and to give the reader a clearer picture. The very possible way we can describe a Cricut machine is to say that it is a machine that has so much resemblance with the printer, but it is used majorly for cutting designed pieces. That is a straightforward and easy definition you do not need to bother yourself about that. Just picture a printer in your mind and think of a cutting device. If you already have the Cricut machine with you. You would notice that it uses precise blades and several templates or rollers during cutting.

Against what people think. The machine is not meant for scrapbook keepers or makers alone. We still do not know why this idea has become so much rooted in the minds of people that we have grown to allow this thought to dominate our reactions and attitude towards any innovation.

The world has been transformed with that machine as its products have been able to add those unique visual beauties to the simple paperwork that we know. The Cricut machine has several models and versions some of them include Cricut Expression, Expression 2, Cricut Imagine, Cricut Gypsy, Cricut Cake Mini, Cricut Personal Cutter, Cricut Crafts Edition and Martha Stewart and the Cricut Explore Air. The tool fits into any type of craft you are working on. And there is also a die-cut machine which gives you that extra-precise, sharp, and smart cutting. The process of cutting materials by hand during crafts has been reduced drastically. More also, you can perform multiple projects all at the same time due to the effectiveness of this device. It contains several cartridges that are always available to help you explore different forms and shapes of several designs. More also that move from one project to another has been made possible with the use of this Cricut machine.

Any material can be shaped into that design you want it to be. Furthermore, you can also create patterns that are already pre-installed in the software that comes with it. The design software tool becomes very much available with pre-loaded designs for instant use. We are sure you must have been able to purchase this machine from your local craft store on the online store. You are aware that the price was based on the kind of model you are using and we are sure that you've been able to narrow down your needs for you to be able to get your machine because anything which makes your work easier and faster is a significant investment and the Cricut machine is one. Due to the efficiency of this machine, we now have it in several places we never thought. We have them in offices and specific workshops. If you feel that the Cricut is a home-only tool, you are entirely wrong. This time-saving device allows your work to be very professional, and the beautiful thing about it is that we have no limits to what it can do. We are sure that you are reading this to gain more ideas and you hastily want to jump into making things and doing some stuff. Yes, that is cool; however, we need to understand some basics else we would be making serious mistakes, or the process would look very confusing.

1.1 Cricut Machine

Cutting machine is a Cricut that can be used for different projects of crafting. It takes projects that you make or submit into their software of design space and cuts them. It sounds easy but we guarantee you'll be surprised by how many things you can do in very less time you'd be willing to accomplish it by hand. We're talking about sewing patterns, calendar stamps, for home wooden labels, mugs monogrammed, and a lot of different things.

This device is great for the imaginative individual who still needs to do projects like DIY but has a limited time to wait on the page of your Pinterest. Also, whether you've got a home-built company or Etsy store, we will pretty much make sure you get much profit from the device.

1.2 Cricut Working

You can wirelessly connect this machine to your laptop, build or export designs to your laptop, and submit them for cutting to the Cricut. Cricut has design space software (available for MAC Windows, and smartphone) that let you in creating and importing cutting designs with your computer. Inside the Cricut, there is a small blade (or scoring tool, or pen, or rotary cutter). Once a material you have that is ready to be cut in the Design Space, add the desired material to a 12" wide cutting pad, transfer your design wirelessly from the computer or laptop to the Cricut, and then the material is loaded in your machine. Your project should begin cutting with a click of a button.

1.3 Types of Cricut machines

In the market, three forms of the Cricut machines are there currently. Cricut Joy (this one just came out), Cricut Maker, and Cricut Explore Air II. Choosing which device, you need to purchase would rely on the kind of project you choose to create. All devices come with free software Design Space.

Explore Air 2 Cricut

For most projects, this device we would consider purchasing. It is the most common machine from Cricut, and it can cover most of the materials you can need for a broad range of projects DIY such as vinyl, cardstock, paper, and chipboard. With this device, you can cut more than 100 items, and use 4 methods to hack, compose, and score.

Cricut Maker

Cricut maker unit performs all the Explore Air 2 Cricut can do, like cutting heavier or more fragile items such as leather, fabrics, and thin woods. With this unit, more than 300 items can be cut, and use more than 12 devices for cutting, scoring, writing, and other effects pro-level. If you decide to delve into more complex ventures and play with a broader variety of products, we will suggest this machine.

Cricut Joy

Cricut Joy, the new Cricut machine, is a further compact machine for simple, daily DIY projects, then the other machines. Materials can be cut up to 5.5" wide only but long material (around 20 feet) you can buy. More than 50 items it cuts and can utilize two tools for writing and cutting. If you would like to invest less and for simple project creation like vinyl posters, cards, and little iron-on patterns, we will suggest this tool.

1.4 What is inside the Cricut box

- Power Cord

- Instruction booklet

- USB Cord (if you are not using Bluetooth for the Maker)

- Blade and Housing (already installed on the machine)

- Additional accessories for a small project to learn with

- Accessory Clamp (already installed on the machine)

1.5 Cricut can be used to cut materials

Everyone likes to think of these Cricut machines like vinyl or cutting paper, but the fact is that much stuff can be cut with the Cricut. The Explore Air 2 Cricut will potentially break over 60 styles of materials. Some Cricut machines will cut materials like silk, leather, and even wood as well as paper, vinyl & cardstock. You'll want to switch to the blade deep-cut for better cut consistency with thicker materials.

And with 100x the Explore Air 2 's pressure capacity, the latest Cricut Maker will cut further materials also. Are you looking for a specialty? This has a completely latest rotary blade due to which it is a necessity for seamstresses, who can now plan a job in minutes rather than hours.

1.6 Upload the photos you like

You can upload your photos or some of our free SVG & Me cut files that are already designed to be entirely Cricut Template Space compliant with them.There are all sorts of forms of image files in there. SVGs are the strongest kind, which stands for scalable graphic vector. Essentially, it uses mathematical formulae to construct a point-based representation between sides.

The benefit of this is that you can expand the SVG graphics without having the blurred pixelated look you see in certain forms of images, rendering them perfect to design projects of any scale!

1.7 How to Convert a Picture to SVG

Users create all their SVG cut files and photos, but to show that for every image you find off the internet, you can do so. Take one out for display on a free clip art platform.

Side note: Using offline files is typically good if it is for personal usage (no monetary gain) but still upholding the pictures and terms of copyright. Choose from this web, just a basic flower clip art pic. After saving it to my computer, Go to PNGtoSVG.com, which is completely FREE and submitted the picture where "choose photo" is mentioned.Scroll down to see the picture surface after you've uploaded it. You'll then use the plus or minus button to raise or decrease the number of colors. When submitted to

Cricut, note that each color should reflect one sheet.First, click on the green 'download SVG' button on the right side underneath your image.

1.8 Upload your SVG to Cricut Design Space

You can typically find the file in the Downloads folder of your device. Navigate to the archive folder and add the SVG to your Development Space in Cricut.

Voilà, voila! You have now transformed a static picture into a flexible 2-layer vector graphic which can now be cut out in several layers! Wasn't it as simple as pastry eating? And now you're feeling super crafty awesome! And this opens so much space to broaden your archive of pictures!

Seeking freebies and purchasing Cricut Exposure are excellent ways to get Web Room SVG data. But what is it to make your own?After all, we must often carry a specific dream to the existence or personalize an object. Inkscape is a free open source software that can be downloaded from scratch to create SVG files or transform photos into layered SVG files.

1.9 DIY projects we can do with the Cricut

Honestly, maybe the greatest and most daunting aspect of purchasing the Cricut is that you don't know to proceed from which point as it is so flexible. So, resist overloading details, and try focusing at a time on a single project.

About Cricut projects, the funny thing is that we will think of unlimited projects before beginning, or see a few of them on Pinterest, and say "oh, they want to do that! "Then, as they sit to create a proposal, the mind will go blank at that moment!

Ok, we have many Cricut projects in this book to assist with this. You can try them out, select one of them from the book, and get workmanship flat in no time.

Where to search for projects?

Cricut Design Space is one of the greatest areas to locate Cricut designs and cut images. If you're designing something from scratch or utilizing a pre-designed layout, this is where all of the Cricut projects launch. Registering a

Cricut Design Space account is easy, and you can use that to test all the available designs or work from home on a product. However, most of the pre-designed project files in

Cricut cost money to use, unless you have a Cricut Access subscription.

Thankfully, the Library gives you your service. If you're using one of our computers and logging into a dedicated Library device, you'll have full access to several of the Design Space ventures, as well as a massive graphic and font database to support you build anything you can come up!

In Design Space, you can even create and use your files.jpg,.gif,.png. ,bmp. , SVG. and.dxf. You may either use photos you have, or buy cut files on places like Etsy, and then add them to the system. Cricut has provided some clear guidance on how to do this on their website.

1.10 Generate earnings from Cricut project

People think the Cricut machine is the one instrument that is responsible for conceptualizing the designs we see in scrapbooks. Ultimately, the prototypes crime from the user's imagination and the Cricut rotting machine renders them visible. However, many resources help you build designs such as adapters and coding applications The most popular digital platform out there is the Cricut Design Studio Using this program, you develop and modify your designs and alter current pre-loaded designs. Life is still nice. People often believe the usage of a Cricut cutting machine is restricted only to the scrap hooking environment. Not many people are aware of this because there the Cricut device can be used for several items along with the cartridges and the program devices. There are several Cricut tasks for which you can use the Cricut cutting machine and what you can do can be restricted only by your imagination. Greeting cards are perfect Cricut creations to communicate with anyone. You build covers that challenge the unusual with the templates that you can get with the Cricut cartridge and the tech resources that you've in place. The dilemma that customers encounter when purchasing holiday cards in malls is that much of the time, they can't locate the card style they're searching for. These on-street cause and much irritation on the part of the customer. You are much better off making your greeting cards. Cricut calendars are a perfect idea for a Cricut cutting system too. Twelve months make up a year. You may get sentimental and search for designs that will represent the month inside your calendar in your program or cartridge. In December month you should search for projects that suit the December mood and environment. Snowmen's novel, reindeers, and Christmas trees. We promise you to have all the designs within your app or cartridge you'll ever like. Know, what you do will be confined to only your imagination. Such Cricut privets may be used for purposes of personal gratification or revenue production. Be imaginative with your machine. You never know what insane and wild thoughts will spring up in your brain.

1.11 Cricut Access subscription and difference with Cricut Design Space

Cricut Access and Cricut Design Space are two separate products. Design Space is the software you use for project design. Cricut Access is a membership-only program that allows you exposure (and other benefits) to specific designs inside Design Space.

Cricut Access is a subscription-based program allowing you to have unrestricted access to over 50,000 images, over 1000 designs and fonts.

The option is between two separate groups. You will pay for each amount on a monthly or annual basis (the annual fee is cheaper than monthly payments).

Membership Monthly:

For the Monthly Membership, you have access to over 400 fonts that are available to go on your Cricut device, access to the Premium Member support system for quick assistance when you need it, unrestricted usage of over 30,000 Cricut images, including unique ones, 10% discounts for all approved fonts, photographs, and available-to-make creations, and 10% off all Cricut.com product orders.

Membership Annual:

Annual Registration is the next step up for membership. The yearly membership is the same as the monthly except available at a reduced rate on an annual basis. With the Yearly Subscription, you have access to over 400 fonts that are ready to go on your Cricut device, access to the Priority User support line for quicker assistance when you need it, unrestricted usage of over 30,000 Cricut images, including unique ones, 10% discounts for all approved fonts, photos, and ready-to-make creations, and 10% off all Cricut.com merchandise transactions.

Membership Premium:

Premium Membership is the highest standard of Cricut Access available. Premium Membership allows you access to over 400 ready-to-use fonts on your Cricut computer, access to the

Preferred Membership service line for quicker help when you need it, unrestricted usage of over 30,000 Cricut images, including unique ones, 10% discounts for all approved fonts, photos, and ready-to-make creations, and 10% off all Cricut.com software orders.

Whether you intend to purchase more than a handful of designs a month, or if you frequently order items from Cricut's website, you'll want to pick up a membership.If a Cricut Access subscription contains a picture, project, or font it will have a green "an" at the top corner. When an object is included in the Cricut Access subscription, it would state.The green Cricut Access banner should light up whether you have a Cricut Access account. You can find it says "Subscribed" so, if you have an Access account, you will use it without charging anything extra. If you don't have an Entry card, you can always purchase the designs but it's going to be a separate fee.When your Cricut Access license ends and you do not want to extend it, you will no longer have Cricut Access photos accessible through your account. This covers something you've accomplished for Access projects before that you intend to do now. All photos, fonts, or creations that you have bought will also stay in your wallet, even though you have the Cricut

Access Discount because bought templates are yours to hold. Cricut Access auto-renews, so if you don't want to renew your order automatically please contact Cricut or cancel it via your Cricut account.

Chapter No.2 Full Cricut Design Space Tutorial for Beginners

Looking to learn more about Cricut Design Space but you don't even know where to start?

Learning a new activity or talent will initially be daunting. We don't know where to start sometimes because there's so much material out there and that's just frustrating.

The easiest way to know and practice Cricut Design Space for everyone is right from the outset. You know, when you have a good idea about what every symbol and panel is about, then you can dive in and start playing on and off.

Often, we 're quick hopping from project to project – Yeah, that's cool too – but we hope learning your field of work would help you push your imagination to a different stage.

Let's know what the Cricut Creative Space Canvas Area is before we dive in.

Once you cut your designs, the Cricut Creative Space Canvas region is where all the fun occurs.

Design Space is where you touch up your designs and arrange them. Not only can you use and upload your fonts and photos in this gallery, but you can also use the premium photos and fonts offered by Cricut by individual transactions, Cricut Access, and Cartridges.

When you don't know how to practice Design Space, investing in a Cricut is pointless, as you will still use this program to cut every product.

Cricut Design Space is a perfect resource for beginners, so if you don't have much background in any other modeling applications like Photoshop or Illustrator, you'll find it's fairly simple though it seems daunting.

When someone can do it, you can do it too!

On the other side, whether you have experience previewing in some of the Adobe Creative Cloud or Inkscape applications. You can see it's only a breeze through this plan. Project Room, this is largely about reaching the ideas and making simple templates of shapes and fonts.

2.1 Design space and membership access

Across your screen, you'll see the tiny Cricut icon and you can press it to launch the software.

Design Space is the application Cricut uses, so it has pre-loaded tasks so files for you to use.

You'll see some of them are safe and others paid. Once you

enter Membership, you'll have 3 separate choices to select from which the subscription price is well worth. If you've shopped for SVGs, you'll note they will vary from $1 to $10 or more for one file only!

Here are the choices which you may pick from:

You can do anything from a window named CANVAS when you log in to your Cricut Design Space account and decide to launch or update a new project.

Cricut Production Space's Canvas Field is where you perform all the editing before you cut down on the designs.

There are so many keys, choices, and stuff you might feel committed to doing. Don't worry, we're here along the way to cheer you up and inspire you to start.

You're about to discover in this book what EVERY SINGLE ICON on the Canvas region is about. We must split the canvas into four regions and four colors to hold it in order and to be quick to understand:

- Editing Area- Top Panel Yellow

- Insert Area- Left Panel Blue

- Layers Panel- Right Panel Purple

- White Canvas Area

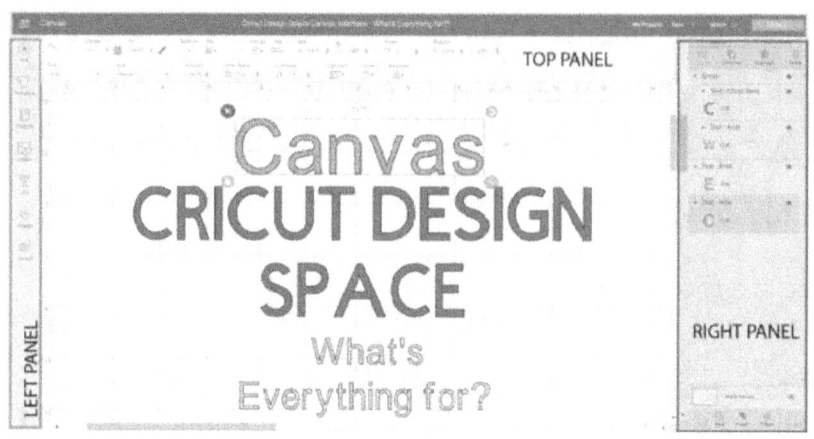

2.2 Cricut Design Space Top Panel

The top panel in the field Project Space Canvas is for editing and organizing objects in the field of the canvas. You can select from this panel which sort of font you'd like to use; you can adjust sizes, match designs, and more!

This row is split down into two subpanels. The first one helps you to save your designs, label them, and eventually cut them. And the second one will enable you to monitor and edit canvas-area stuff.

2.3 Subpanel # 1Name Your Project and Cut it

This sub-panel helps you to navigate to your profile, projects from the Canvas and it even takes you to split your finished projects.

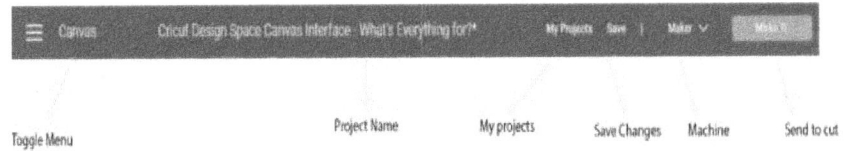

Toggle Menu

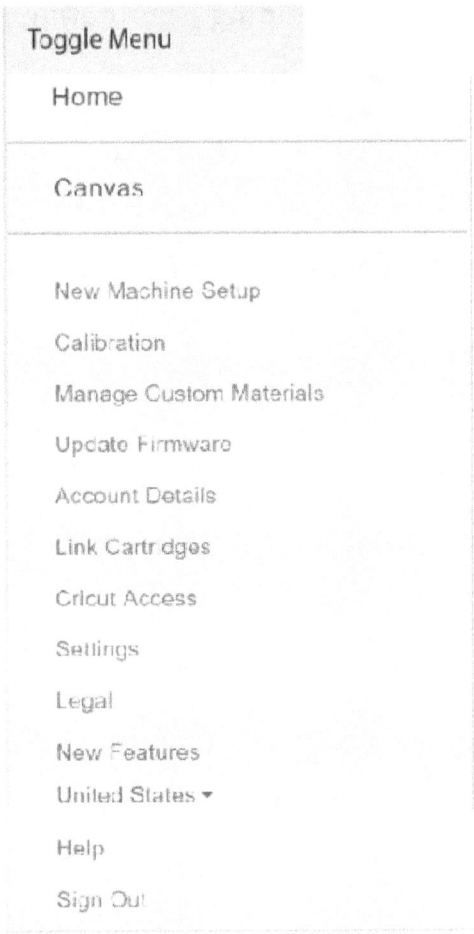

Clicking on the button will open another entire line. This menu is convenient. So, it's not part of the Canvas, so that's why there is no need to go into any depth.

You can essentially go to your profile from here and adjust your picture.

Through this Menu there is other helpful and technological stuff you can do including calibrating, blades; and upgrading your device's firmware – app.

Note: You can adjust the visibility and dimensions of the Canvas on the Settings option; this is best described at the end of this article where we clarify more about the canvas area.

Name of Project

Both projects start with a * Untitled "title," after you have put at least one item (Image, form, etc.) you can only call a project from the canvas field.

My Projects

Once you click on my projects, the items you've already made will be forwarded to your library; that is perfect because occasionally you may like to re-cut an item that was already produced. Therefore, you do not need to do the same idea again and again.

Save This

This choice will trigger after one item has been put on your canvas field. It is strongly recommended that you save the idea while you go. Because if the app is in the cloud, if the browser crashes, the good work on it goes!

Maker – Explorer (Machine)

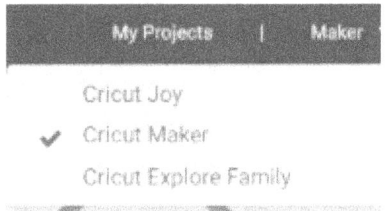

You would need to pick either the Cricut Joy, the Maker, or the Cricut Explore Machine based on the type of device you have; this is necessary as you can have features on the Cricut Maker which are only accessible on that specific machine.

But, if you've got a Maker and you're building ON with the Explore method, you're not going to be able to enable the creator software.

The line type choices are different.

Let it possible.

When your files are saved, and ready to cut press create it!

You will also raise the number of tasks to remove through that window; this is perfect if you intend on making more than one break.

Only click on Build it. All you think is this.

2.4 Subpanel # 2-Editing Menu

It's incredibly helpful and can help you scan, organize, and coordinate fonts and photographs in the Canvas field.

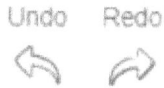

Undo& Redo

Often, we make errors as we work. Such small keys are an ideal way to fix them.

When you build anything, you don't want or making an error, press Undo. When you unintentionally remove something that you do not intend to remove or alter, press Redo.

Linetype and Fill

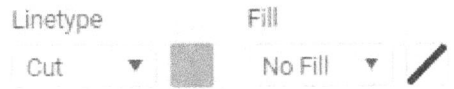

This choice would inform your computer which equipment and blades you'll be using.

Bear in mind that you'll have various choices based on the Computer you chose at the top of the window (Maker or Explore).

Linetyping

This choice would inform you about what device you would be using while you are cutting your job. There are seven choices in a position right now (Cut, Draw, Engrave, Score Deboss, Perf, Wave).

When you have a Cricut Builder, both choices are open, so if you have an Explore, you just have the option Cut, Draw, and Rate.

Below is an overview of each resource in greater detail.

Cut

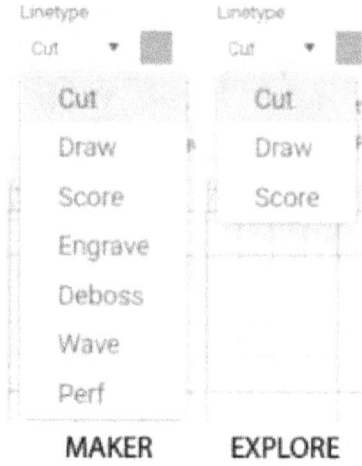

MAKER   EXPLORE

If you've submitted a JPEG or PNG file to the Canvas; "Cut" is the default line type any of the components would have on the canvas; that ensures that when you click MAKE IT, the device must cut certain designs.

You will adjust the fill of the components with the Cut choice chosen, at the end of the day that transforms into the various shades and products that you can use while cutting the designs.

Draw

You should do that with your Cricut if you want to write in your sketches!

When issuing this line type, you'll be asked to pick either of the Cricut Pens you have (unless you have a 3rd party converter, you require different pens). The layers on your canvas region will be highlighted with the color of the pen you selected while choosing a specific style.

Using this method, the Cricut can compose or sketch if you press Create it, instead of cutting. Note: Paint the designs, not with this choice.

Score

This is a more powerful Scoring line variant positioned on the left side. If this characteristic is applied to a sheet both designs should appear scored and dashed.

This time, clicking on Create it. Your Cricut won't break, but your materials will score.

You'll need the scoring stylus or the scoring wheel for certain kinds of designs. Bear in mind, however, the wheel functions only with the Cricut Manufacturer.

Engrave, Deboss, Wave, and Perf (New)

Those are the newest devices Cricut has launched for the Cricut Maker device, so you will be able to make incredible results on various content styles using them.

Fill in

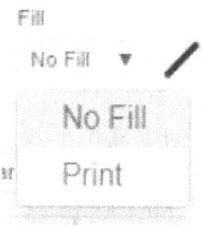

The fill alternative is to be used exclusively for printing and patterning.

Only after you have cut as a "line type" should it be allowed. No Fill ensures you won't print it out.

Printing is by far, one of Cricut's greatest features as it helps you to print the designs and then edit them down; that is awesome, and frankly, that's what inspired me to get a Cricut first.

People create lots of printable for kiddos and adults, so they had to cut every single little item to take pictures – for blogs!

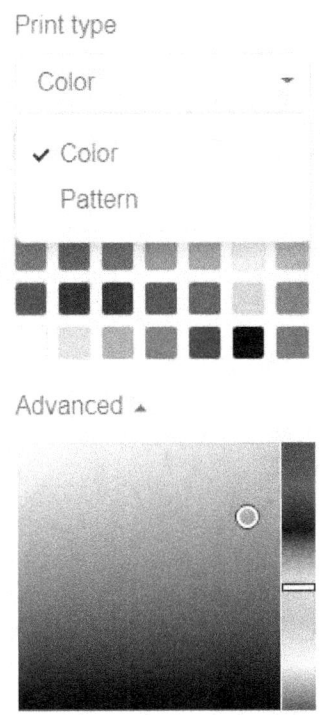

We get back to the Print alternative anyway. After you press Render it when this Fill choice is active; you can submit your files to your home printer first and then let your Cricut do all the heavy lifting. (Cutting)

Another fantastic print choice is Patterns!!! that's just too great. Using the choices Cricut makes or upload your own; you can apply a template to almost any sheet.

Print type

Pattern   ▼

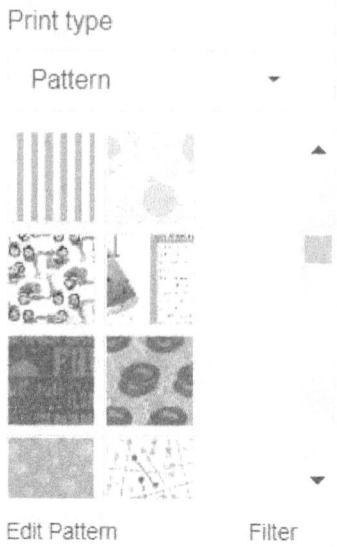

Edit Pattern   Filter

Let's just say today is Valentine's Day. You can make a gorgeous card from Cricut Access (Membership, not free), or your own, with a template already made. And at the same time print out and break.

Edit Pattern

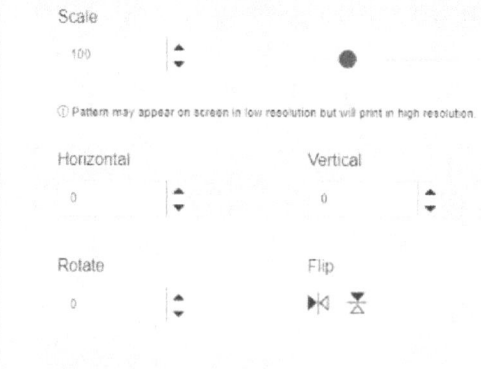

To suit your needs, update your patterns!

Select All

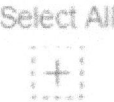

You might be struggling to pick them one by one as you try to transfer all the elements within the canvas field.

Select choose all items from the canvas to pick everything.

Edit

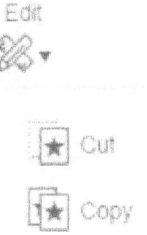

This icon will allow you to cut (remove from the canvas), copy (copy the same thing, leaving the original intact), and paste objects from the canvas (insert copied or cut elements in the canvas area).

The Icon edit has a drop-down menu.

Once you have a collection of one or more items from the canvas region, the cut and copy choice are disabled. When you copy or cut anything the Paste alternative will be available.

Align

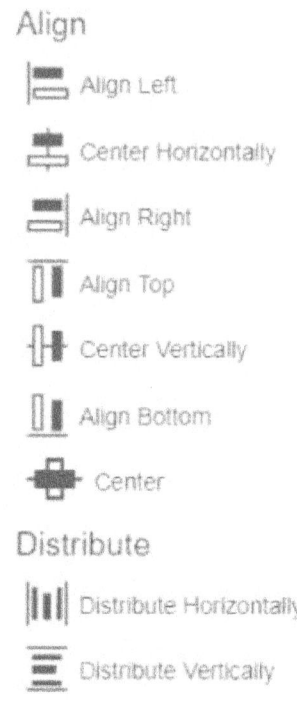

Align

- Align Left
- Center Horizontally
- Align Right
- Align Top
- Center Vertically
- Align Bottom
- Center

Distribute

- Distribute Horizontally
- Distribute Vertically

Its features help you to coordinate all your projects, and when you choose two or more components it is enabled.

– Left align: Both components must be moved to the left by using this configuration. The furthest element to the left determines where all the other components are going to move forward.

– Center Horizontal: This choice would place the items horizontally; the text and photographs would be centered completely.

– Align Right: Each of the components should be positioned to the right while you use this configuration. The furthest element to the right determines where all the other components are going.

– Align Top: This choice aligns all your selected designs to the top. The furthest factor up to the top determines where all the other components pass.

– Vertically centered: This choice aligns the components vertically. If you're dealing with columns, it's convenient and you want them to be ordered and coordinated.

– Align Bottom: This choice aligns with all the designs you've picked to the floor. The furthest factor down to the bottom determines where all the other components pass.

– Center: Extremely cool choice. Once you click on "center," you center one pattern against another, both vertically and horizontally; this is especially helpful if you choose to center text with a form like a square or a circle.

Distribute

When you want the same arrangement for components, doing that all on your own is time-consuming, and it's not

100 percent accurate. It will help you out with the Distribute release. You must have at least three elements chosen for it to be allowed.

- Horizontally distribute: This press distributes the components horizontally. The furthest left and right designs would decide the allocation length; this implies that the products in the middle will be divided to the farthest left and right designs.

- Vertically distribute: This click will spread the components upside down. The furthest top and bottom designs would decide the extent of the distribution; this involves dividing the products in the middle of the most remote top and bottom designs.

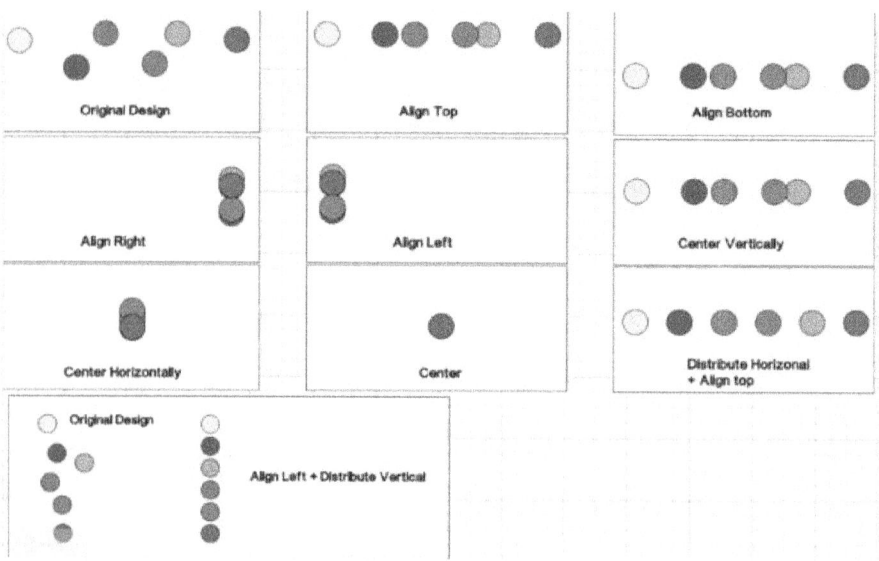

Arrange

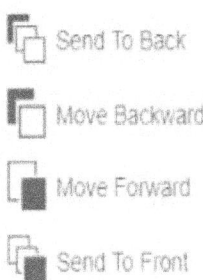

Send To Back

Move Backward

Move Forward

Send To Front

If dealing with numerous pictures, words, and templates, the latest ideas you are bringing to the canvas will still be in front of everyone. Many of the concept components ought to be in the back or front, however.

You can organize the elements very quickly using the arrange method.

Another nice aspect of this feature is that the system knows what object is on the front or back, so when you pick it, design space will trigger the choices available for that specific product.

These are your options:

– Send back: It takes the selected item all the way backward.

– Backward movement: this choice pushes the chosen object

only one step back. When you have a concept of three components, instead. It's going to feel like the bacon in a sandwich.

– Going Forward: this choice will push the object one stage forward. This choice will usually be utilized when you have four or more things that you need to organize.

– Send to front: This choice transfers the chosen object to the front.

Flip

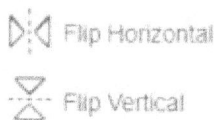

When you choose to show some of your Cricut Design Space designs this is a perfect way to do it.

There are 2 possibilities:

– Horizontal flip: This will horizontally represent the picture or concept. Kind of like a mirror; it's useful as you want to build patterns to the left and right. Example: you create some wings, and you already have the left side; you can copy and paste the left wing with Flip, and voila! Already all of you (left and right) have wings!

– Vertical flip: It should turn the projects upside down. Yeah, sort of like you'd see the water image. The choice will be perfect for you if you want to build a shadow effect.

Size

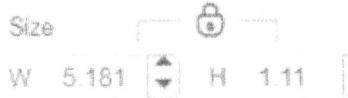

There's a size of anything you make or form in Cricut Design Space. You will self-adjust the size of the item (when you click on it). Nevertheless, this choice helps you to do so if you require an object to have an exact measurement.

The tiny lock is something important. As the size of a picture rises or reduces, the proportions are still fixed. You inform the system by clicking on the little lock that you don't want to have the same measurements.

Rotate

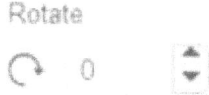

As with size, rotating an item from the canvas region is something you can do very easily. Many projects ought to be switched to a different angle, however. If this is the case with you, we would suggest that you use this feature. Or you'll waste too much time trying to make an angled item the way you want it to be.

Position

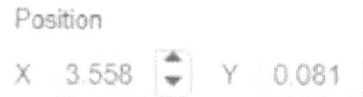

The box tells you when you click on a template, where your things are on the canvas field.

Through deciding where you want the item to be placed on the canvas areas you may shift the items around. It's useful but it's a more advanced device.

Honestly, people don't use it too often because the alignment methods described above help them to move around easier.

Font

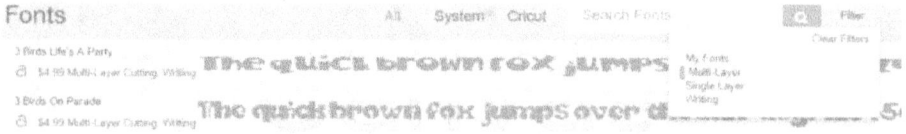

Clicking on this panel will require you to pick any font you want to use for your projects. You will scan them on top of the browser, then check for them.

When you have Cricut Access, you can use all the fonts at the beginning of the font description which has a little green A.

However, if you don't have connections to Cricut, make sure you use the fonts in your system; else you'll be fined when you submit a cut to your project.

Style

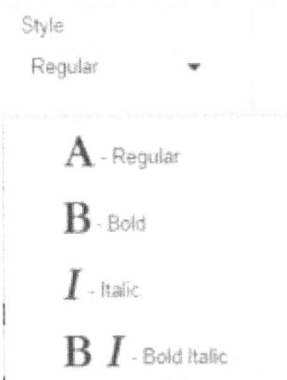

When the font is chosen, you have the choice to alter its type.

You have several options:

Regular: this is the default configuration, which does not change the font appearance.

Bold: Make the text bigger.

Italic: The font is going to turn to the right.

Bold italic: it should thick the text and turn to the right.

Font Size, Letter & Line Space

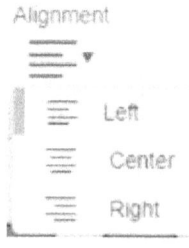

Font Size	Letter Space	Line Space
60 1	VA 1 2	1 2

Font Size: From here, you can adjust it manually. We typically just change the thickness of the canvas region of the fonts.

Letter Space: The distance between each letter is substantial in certain fonts. This choice would cause you to very easily will the space between the letters. This is a game-changer.

Line Space: this method would fix the distance between lines in a paragraph; this is quite helpful as often required to construct a single line of text when someone might not be satisfied with the spacing between lines.

Alignment

Alignment

Left

Center

Right

This Alignment is distinct from the other "alignment"

above. For paragraphs, the choice is.

Those are your options:

- Left: Left Align the paragraph

- Centre: align the section to the middle

- Right: fit a section to Right

Curve

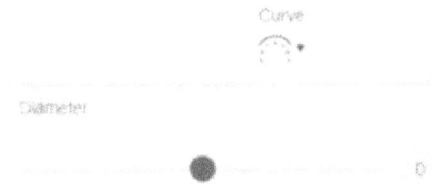

With this alternative, you can get extra creative with your text!

You will curve the text with this function — the easiest way to practice this is by playing with the little slider.

When shifting the lever to the west, the text will be bent upwards; while by pushing it to the back, it will turn the text inwards.

Note: if you shift the slider completely to the left or the right; with your fonts, you can shape a circle.

Advance

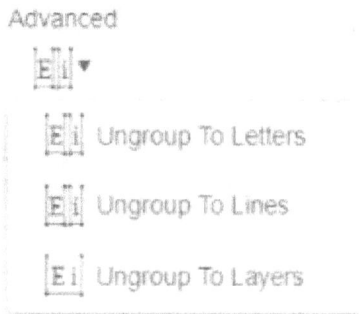

Advance is the last editing-panel option.

Don't be fooled by the drop-down menu word. When you know what all the tools are about, you'll find that they aren't too complicated to use.

– Ungroup letters: this choice helps you to split each letter into a single layer (clarify layers below); use this if you're going to alter each character.

– Ungroup to Lines: This choice is excellent and enables you to isolate a paragraph from each section. Type the sentence, then press to line ungroup and you've got it there; a new line that you can now change.

– Ungroup to Layers: this one is the trickiest of all such possibilities. This choice is not available for Multi-Layer fonts; these fonts are eligible only for individual transactions and, or Cricut Access.

A multilayer font is a type of font that has more than one layer; if you want any shadow or color around it, such fonts are fantastic.

How if you want a multi-layer template, just don't want the layer added? Simply pick the text and then click on layer ungroup to split every single sheet.

Left Panel – Insert Shapes, Images & More.

2.5 Left Panel

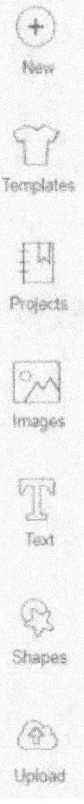

You will edit all the templates with the top panel (that has already been clarified in detail).

Yet where are they all coming from? They all come from the Left Panel at Cricut Design Space.

This panel is mostly about adding shapes, photos, projects ready to cut, and more. Starting here you'll be removing all of the stuff you'll remove.

There are seven choices for this Panel:

- New: The design and installation of a new canvas project.

- Templates: this helps you to get a reference about what kinds of items you'll remove. Let's assume you'd like to iron an onesie on vinyl. You will plan and see how the product will appear as you select the prototype.

- Projects: Install the Cricut Access software cut set.

- Images: Select single pictures from Cricut Access and make project cartridges.

- Text: To apply the text to your canvas field click here.

- Shapes: Bring shapes into the canvas.

- Uploads: upload photos to the system, then split data.

There's something fundamental to remember on this panel;

when you've got Cricut Control, Cricut Pictures, ready to cut programs, and cost money for Cricut fonts. You would have to compensate for using them until you cut the bid.

So, because on this side we had a little taste of what it all was about. Let's see what occurs when every one of those keys is turned on.

New

Once you press Open, even if you're still working on a project, you'll get a message at the top of the window telling you whether you want to change the item.

Make sure to keep all the modifications from the latest project if you decide to substitute the idea; else you will miss all the good work. A brand new and unused canvas should open after you save for you to get going.

Templates

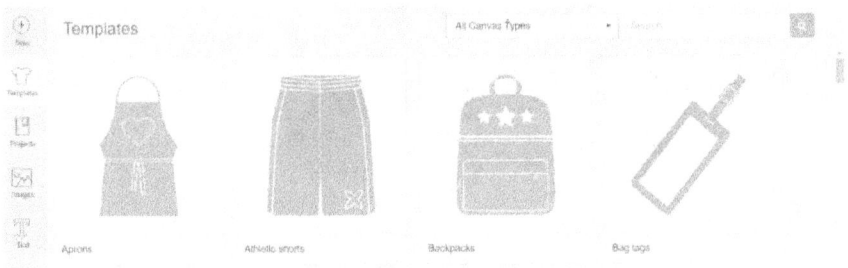

Templates let you see and see if the idea works on a defined surface

If you choose to design fashion pieces, this device is great, since you can select sizes for various garment styles. And they do have several specific types from which to select.

Projects

When you decide to cut straight away, otherwise you want to move to Works! You may configure the project after you have picked it or click on render it and obey the cutting directions.

Tip: The bulk of the projects are open to members of Cricut Membership, or you can purchase them as you travel. There is also a range of designs, FREE to cut based on the computer you've got. Just navigate to the drop-down menu at the bottom of the categories and pick the device you possess.

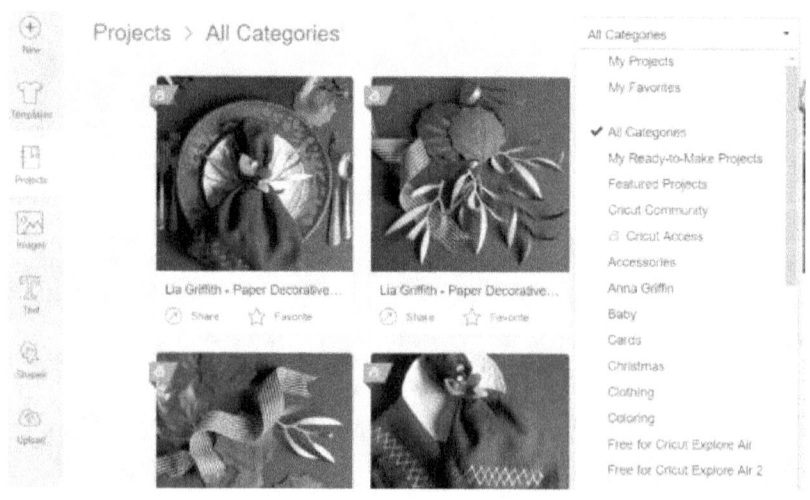

Pictures/Images

When you bring together your creations, the pictures are perfect; with them, you can attach extra touch and personality to your crafts.

You can check through keywords, categories, or cartridges.

Cartridges are a collection of pictures you ought to purchase separately; some come with Cricut Access, and others don't. (Brands such as Disney, Sesame Street, Hello Kitty, etc. Are not part of Cricut Access).

Every week, Cricut has FREE photos to cut. You can reach them by tapping Classes.

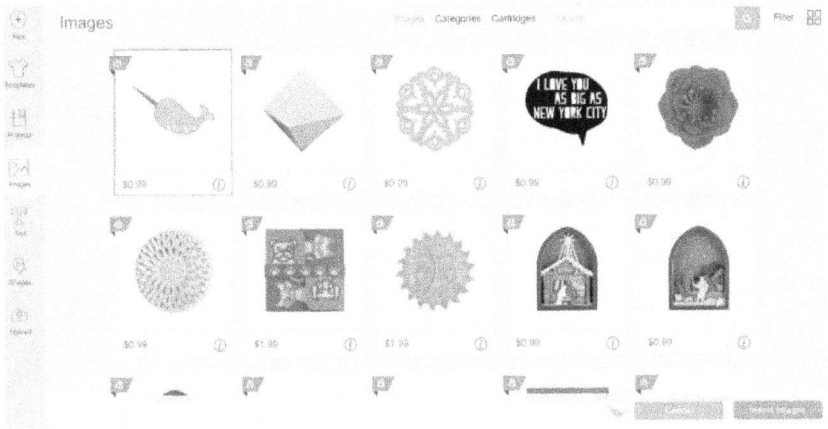

Text

You would need to press Text every time you want to text in the Canvas area; then a tiny window that says Add Text here will appear on the canvas.

Shapes

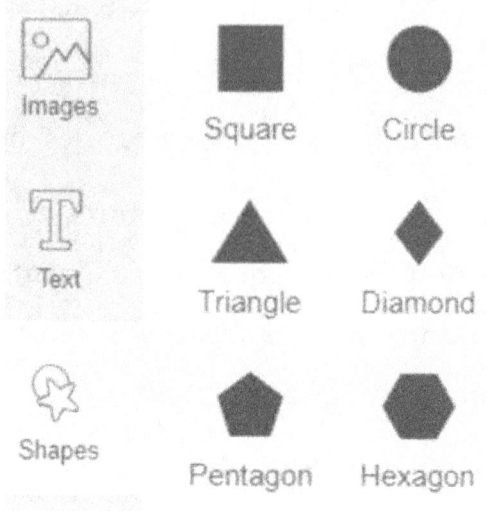

Being able to use forms, it's key! You will build simple and less complex designs with them, and (also) lovely ones.

There're nine forms you may pick from:

- Triangle

- Square

- Hexagon

- Pentagon

- Octagon

- Star

- Heart

The last choice is not a shape, but an extraordinary and efficient tool called the Score Line. You can build folds with this choice and score your materials.

When you want to make boxes or enjoy all about card design, the Score Line would be your best mate!

Upload

Most notably! You can upload your files and photos using this tool. They're loaded with the internet; there are lots of blogs making ideas for free.

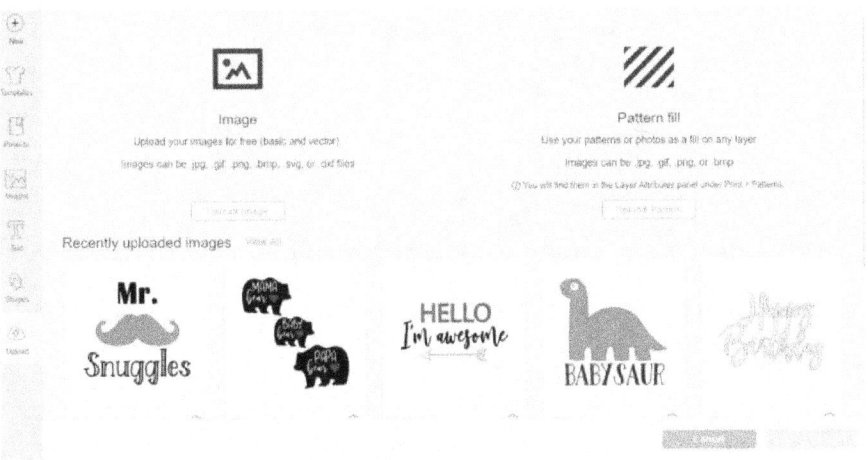

2.6 Right Panel-Know all about layers

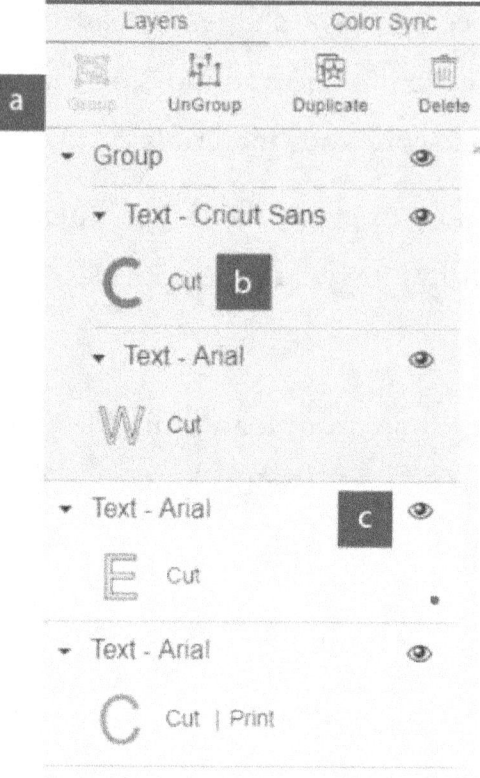

To set you up for success and before we clarify what every symbol on the Layers Panel is all about, let's send you a little overview of what a layer is.

The layer represents any single item or design on the canvas region.

Think of it as clothing; as you get ready, you've got several fabrics that make up your outfit; and your outfit can be easy or complicated based on the day or time of year.

Then the garments will be jeans, trousers, sweater, scarf, hat, boots, gloves, etc. on a cold day; then for a day at the beach, you will just have one coat, a Swimsuit!

The same occurs for design; you may have various styles of levels, based on the nature of the project you are working on, that will make up the whole project.

Let's imagine you are creating a Christmas card for starters.

Which type of token does this have?

Perhaps a text that says Merry Christmas, a flower, the card itself, maybe an envelope too?

The argument is all the tiny drawings and components that make up this project are layers.

Many layers may be modified; but, certain layers, such as photos from JPEG and PNG, cannot; this is due to the existence of the format or the layer itself.

For example, a layer of text may be translated into certain forms of layers; but as you do that, you may lack the right to modify the document.

When you continue, you'll hear more about what layers can or can't do.

Hope you know exactly what a sheet is! Now let's know

what every single icon on this right panel is about.

Group, Ungroup, Duplicate and Delete

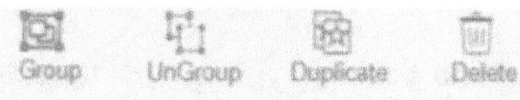

Such settings should make it easier for your life to push stuff across the canvas field, so make sure you mess around with them.Group: To combine the layers click here. If you have various layers that make up a complicated architecture, this is useful.Let's presume you work on some elephant. Very definitely (even whether this is an SVG or cut file) the elephant would be made up of various textures (the torso, head, paws, tail, etc.); if you choose to include additional images, even text; more definitely you can push the elephant a lot around the canvas.

Thus, by arranging all the layers of the elephant, you will make sure that it remains ordered and nothing gets out of position as you push them across the canvas instead.

Ungroup: This method ungroups any clustered layers that you choose on the canvas region or panel layers. Using this method if you need to modify a specified item or layer from the community (size, font style, etc.).

Duplicate: This choice duplicates any layers or designs that you chose on the panel or canvas layers.

Delete: This choice will remove any items on the canvas or layers panel that you picked.

Linetype/Fill

r

Each object in the Layers Panel would display whether you are using Linetype or Fill (Cut, Read, Rate, Perf, Wavy, Print, etc.).

Layer Visibility

The little eye on the panel of layers that exists on each sheet shows the appearance of a logo. If you are not sure if an item looks fine, click on the little eye to mask the feature, instead of removing it. Note: If you cover an object, a cross mark may appear on the eye.

Blank Canvas

This "cover" helps you to adjust the color of the canvas as you want to see if it appears like a specific style with a certain hue. If you use it along with the Templates method, the strength of this configuration is released as you can change the color and design choices themselves.

Slice, Connect, Attach, Contour and Flatten

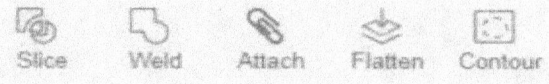

Such instruments that you see here are extremely important! And make sure they are perfected to quality.

The initial template as you can see in the illustration is a pink circle with a teal rectangle. So, let's see what occurs when all those tools are included.

Slice

This slicing tool is appropriate for cutting out various styles of forms, text, and other components.

Once we picked all shapes and pressed on slice, you can see that all of the original files were cut up; to show you what the result was, copied and pasted the "slice outcome" and then removed all of the bits arising from slicing.

Welded

The welding tool lets you merge two or more forms into one.

Attachment

Connect acts like stacking bricks but is better.

Flatten

This tool offers extra help for the setting of Print, then Cut Fill; when you adjust the fill from no fill to print, this only applies to one sheet. So, what if now, you choose to use that with different forms?

When the design is done, pick the layers that you want to print together as a whole, then press on the flatten.

When you're finished with your template (after leaving your task, you can't reverse this), pick the layers you want to print out as a whole and then press on flattening.

In this situation, the item has been a print then cut pattern, so that's why it no longer shows a black edge (where the blade passes through).

Contour

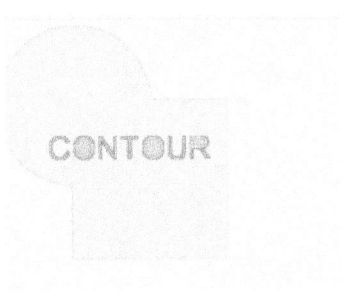

The Contour method helps you to cover unwanted parts of a design, so then where a form or pattern contains components that can be left out can it be enabled.

Color Synchronization

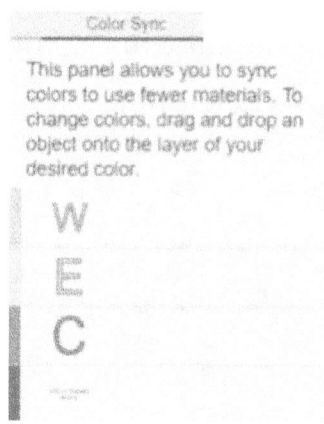

Color Sync is the layers panel's last option.

Per color on your canvas region is a specific color to the content. When there are many shades of yellows or blues in your design; are you confident you need them?

When you need just one yellow hue, as in this case. Just press the tone you want to get rid of and pull it down on the one you want to hold.

2.7 Canvas Area

The space surrounding the canvas is where you display all

the sketches and components. It is intuitive and user friendly!

Canvas Grid and Measurements

A grid separates the canvas area; this is perfect because any little square you see on the grid allows you to see the cutting pad. That will eventually help you optimize your room.

Once you press on the top panel button, you will adjust the dimensions from inches to cm and switch the screen on and off and then choose Preferences.

For all the options a window opens.

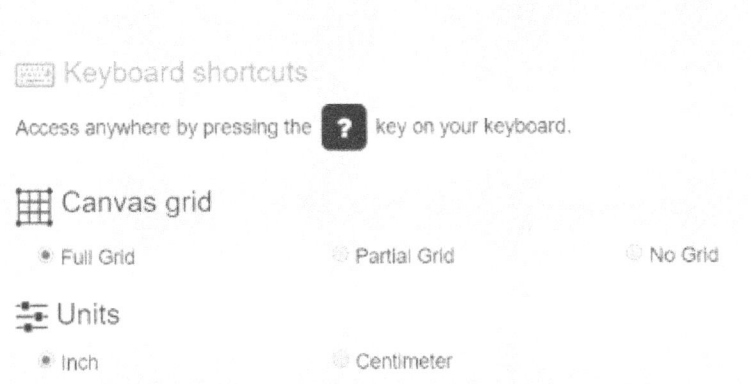

Design Space settings

Keyboard shortcuts

Access anywhere by pressing the **?** key on your keyboard.

Canvas grid

● Full Grid   Partial Grid   No Grid

Units

● Inch   Centimeter

Selection

The array is blue if you pick one or more fabrics, and you

may change it from all four corners.

The "red x" is for the layers to be added. The right upper corner helps you to rotate the picture.

The selection's bottom right clicks, "the little lock," holds the scale equal while growing or reducing the layer thickness. Now you are going to get various proportions by tapping on it.

Zoom out and in

Last but certainly not least. You may do so by clicking the "+ and-" signs on the lower-left corner of the canvas if you choose to display on a greater or smaller scale (without changing the actual size of the designs).

That's it-You're no longer a beginner!

Chapter No. 3 Cricut Design for Beginners

We've put together a collection of simple beginning ideas which are the ideal beginner Cricut projects!

Any of the Cricut projects can be produced in just under a good few hours, using simple materials and basic skills. Steps have been mentioned below that can guide you through the entire cycle of the project from start to finish.

3.1 Face mug

To newcomers, one of the simplest Cricut tasks is simply to cut some vinyl and glue it onto a cup. Easy peasy! That's the Cute Face Mug for starters. You don't think it's adorable?

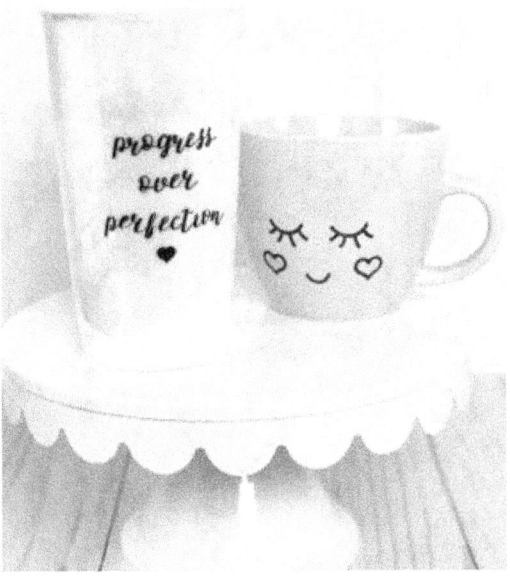

This beginner friendly Cricut project is nothing more than a self-adhesive vinyl that is cut on the Cricut and moved to this mug afterward. You can place vinyl like this with a smooth surface on tons of items — glass, metal, wood, acrylic, plastic, and even canvas! Instead of using iron-on vinyl, the trick here is to use self-adhesive vinyl, often known as art vinyl. You do want to make sure that you have normal transfer tape, not "Strong Grip" transfer tape that's an early error for many other beginners.

3.2 T-shirt-craft

Many people get Cricut because they can create fun T-shirts like this "Making" shirt — and the good news is that you can create T-shirts with your Cricut very fast!

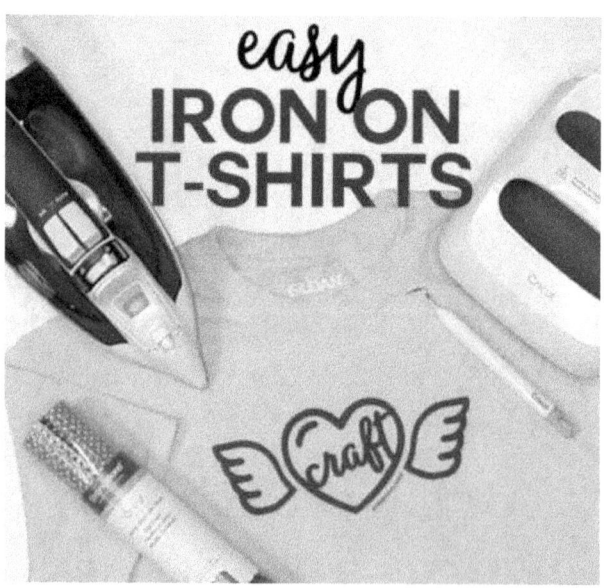

We use iron-on vinyl instead of utilizing self-adhesive vinyl as we did for the mug — often named heat transfer vinyl or HTV. On your Cricut, you easily cut out the logo and add it to the T-shirt. So, this heart style workshop is a perfect idea for working on.

3.3 Cards: peek-a-boo

What about a simple and quick layout on paper? Inspired by the starter card project that comes with new Cricut devices, these basic layered peek-a-boo cards took the idea only one step further:

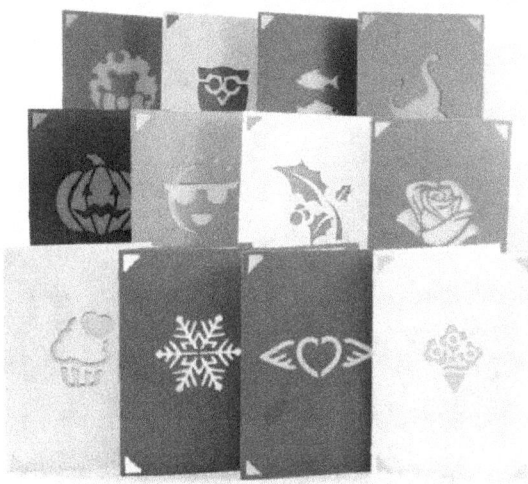

What you need to do for this beginner-friendly project is cut two different cardstock colors, fold one sheet in half and then tie them together — you don't even need glue! There is a total of 24 different designs, so there's one card for each occasion. They even make a perfect gift — many of our fellow designers have brought together the entire greeting card package and offered it to someone who enjoys sending cards. Or just make one for yourself and there's still a wallet on deck. It is one of the best projects for beginners on Cricut!

3.4 Canvas butterfly heart

Here's another paper-based collaboration for all of our amateur crafters a wooden butterfly heart that is a huge success.

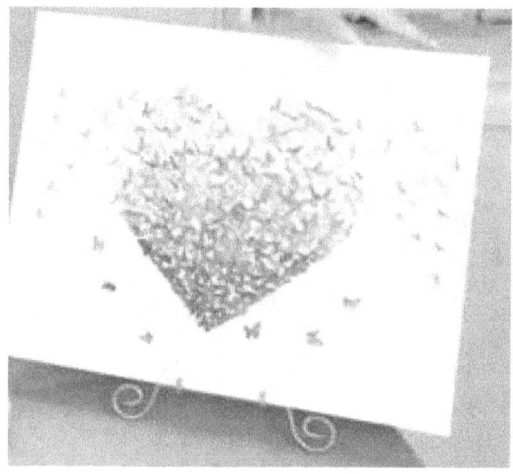

What's so funny about this butterfly project is that it's super easy to make while it looks stunning! It's nothing more than folded paper butterflies, stuck onto a plain white canvas.

Thanks to your Cricut, the butterflies are quick to cut, so you easily fold the wings in half and glue the butterflies on in a heart shape or whatever form you choose! With self-adhesive vinyl, you can also apply a phrase to the canvas which is always easy to do. It is just the great Cricut project for newcomers and everyone's always going to be impressed you've created something yourself.

3.5 Luminary paper or gift package

People are also a huge fan of paper creations as they find them simple to cut and mount. After having Cricut there, they just did paper projects for the first month, because it was simpler. Here's another paper-based idea that transforms simple cardstock into elegant gift boxes or luminaires.

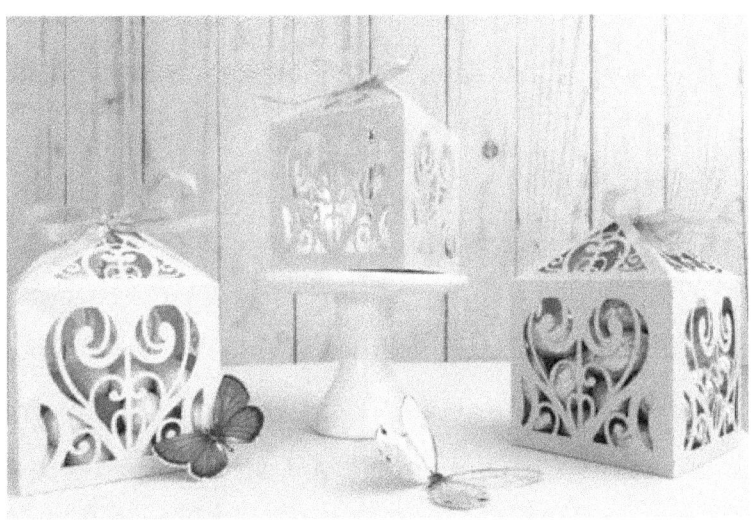

Just cut a sheet of cardstock on your Cricut using my beautiful filigree template for this project. Either easily fold it, glue it or label it, and attach a cord to hold it covered. Now simply tap into it and see it show up in an LED tealight. This project is super simple and has a big wow factor!

3.6 Earring faux leather

Knew you could cut your Cricut and create earrings? These earrings made from leather are super simple and fun!

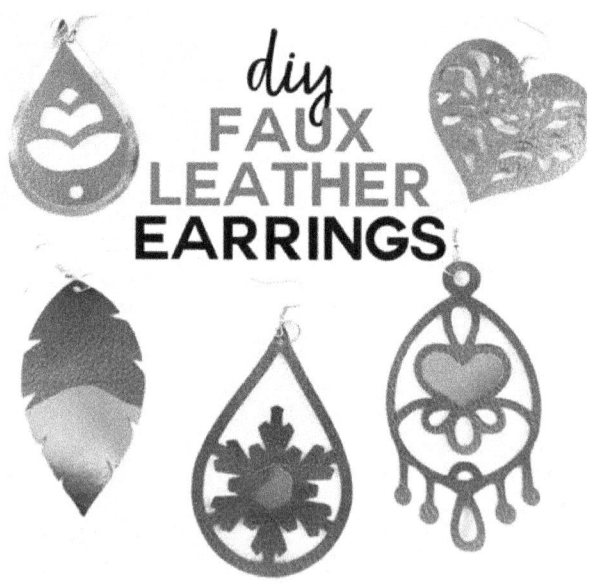

The good thing about fake leather is that it's very super thin which makes cutting on your Cricut very quick. And you can quickly create plain earrings or elegant earrings thanks to the capacity of your Cricut to cut out just about every pattern you want it to. You can also cut the little hole at the top of the earring, and what you need to do is just cut it and place it in the finding of the tube. So facile!! And if you feel up to it, you should put a shiny iron-on vinyl on top of your faux leather-like we did in the earrings above. It is not impossible to do.

3.7 T-shirt personalized

Finally, using Cricut Infusible Ink Transfer sheets, you will learn how to make a simple, customized T-shirt:

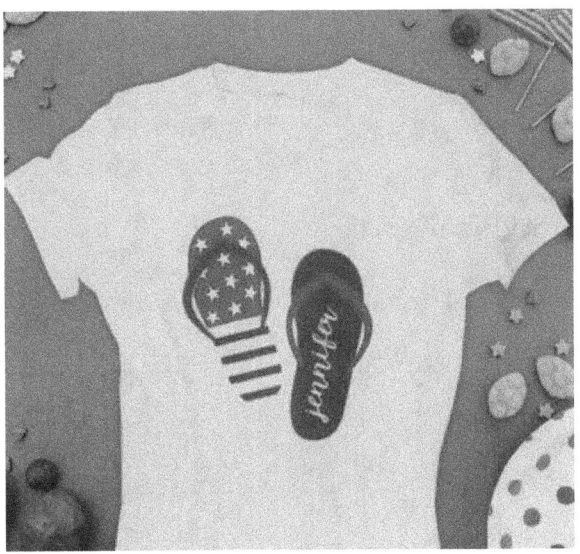

Infusible Ink is easy to work with, producing very colorful designs that last if your shirt. And personalizing with a label, as we did in the above picture, is not hard at all. We'll show you how to attach your name to any picture like this to make a cool and personalized T-shirt that will last a LONG time. We believe Infusible Ink is one of the best novices Cricut projects because of the nice designs you will get in the transfer papers.

3.8 10-minute design toy story bag

It has never been faster or cheaper to produce these.

Supplies for the birthday toy tale favors

- Mint-Machine Profile

- 30X60 mm Frame Stamp

- Stamping Color Black

- Bags favorite

- PNG illustration of space ranger

Next, you will want to use the software of Silhouette Mint to add the image to Mint canvas. When the file has been saved, submit it to the Mint. Once you have pressed to submit, the file will immediately reverse, and it will bring up a sample of what the picture would appear like after it is released.

Through the device run the stamped canvas, and then take the plastic sheet off. Stick it to the block and then to the greyed-out areas of the graphic add the blue ink. Allow the ink to soak in the stamp for at least 15 minutes and now stamp all the extra on the scrap paper piece before you make the image clear.

3.8.1 When to stamp the toy story bag

The block label is stamped until you have drained the excess dye, and then adhere this to the block. Slide a cardstock piece (thick)in the pocket, so that stamp your picture from the showing through seams without lines. Stamp all the bags and then line them with a yummy Popcorn Birthday Cake.

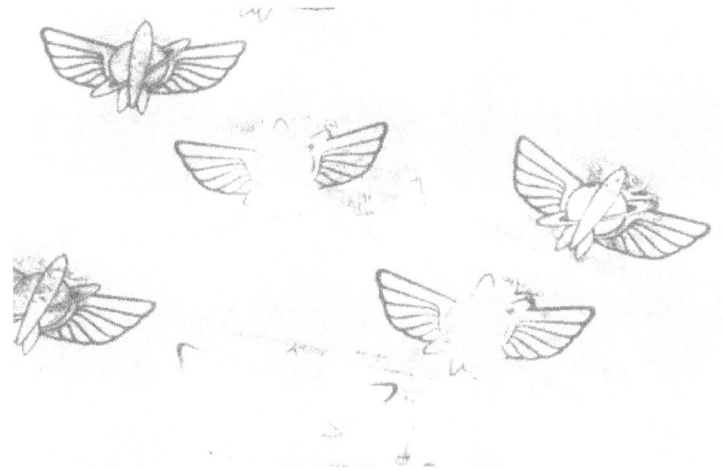

3.9 Quick DIY pumpkin sprinkle

This cute sprinkle pumpkin is the fast and simple project of today! Also, with painting time (excluding drying period), it took less than 15 minutes to render this pumpkin and it is great

Halloween decor for easily spooked family.

This pumpkin is decorated with sprinkles on sticky paper.

DIY supplies of pumpkin

- Plastic Pumpkin

- Color spray (optional)

- Cricut Explore or Maker

- In white, purple, and blue sticky vinyl

- Sprinkles file in Cricut Design Space

DIY pumpkin tips

You should paint your pumpkin if the pumpkin is a color you don't want (our was a country cool white with a brown stem). The color spray was used-far easier than the art project!

Cut the sprinkles on your Cricut Explore or Creator while your pumpkin is drying. Weed out the excess — it will quickly fall up in one piece and leave you with only the sprinkles.

So just take the sprinkles as stickers and put them on your pumpkin. FASHING! The DIY pumpkin is too simple to create!

You will see some details on the Easter t-shirt guide if you need more specific guidance about how to use and cut heat transfer vinyl.

3.10 DIY Coasters on Citrus

Summer Challenge in Cricut.

This is the first formal Cricut "challenge" and the theme was summer. For a Cricut Explore, there are so many things you can do that it was hard to choose only one. So, as we pondered what summer represented one of the first thoughts that came to mind was ice-cold lemonade. We began brainstorming lemonade recipes for the Cricut, which might create. We dropped a coaster on the foot the same day and smashed it (not the foot, the coaster). And that's when we came up with the idea, coasters with citrus fruit!

Those are SO quick to do with your Explore Air; in less than 5 minutes you will create a whole package. What you need are cork coasters.

3.10.1 Guidelines:

- Click to open design in the Design Space.

- Adjust the orientation of the eight triangles such that the circle is all that slices at first (click on the eye next to the triangles in the drop-down menu on the right side to get a slit across the eye).

- Take the white vinyl ring out.

- Centre circle on the coaster and use a scraper tool to insure the coaster is well connected.

- Go back to the interface space and unhide triangles (click again on the eye) and then cover the circle, so that this time only the triangles are removed.

- Be sure to weld the triangles so that they stay in the same place in the design space as you break them (press above the first triangle, move your cursor, build a square across all 8 triangles, then press WELD at the top of the drop-down menu).

- Split 4 pieces of blue, purple, orange, and green triangles one each.

- Within the white circle line up the center of the triangle and use the scraper tool to make sure they are smooth and well connected.

- You now have colorful coasters that will cover your tables and give a color burst to your decor. Those will also make a nice neighbor gift; only purchase a bottle of lemonade and add some bakers' twine to the coasters.

3.11 How to Know That a Beginner project is successful or not

If you've found a pretty impressive project and you're not sure whether it's a decent novice project or if something is completely fresh to you, it is too hard to learn what is successful or not. Here are our expectations for a successful Cricut project for starters:

Instructions: Are there specific instructions for the project? Evite ventures with no clear paths, or those that are so plain. You want to get it laid out for you, and when you get lost you know what to do. For beginners, the best Cricut projects have very simple guidelines, which are broken down step by step.

Materials: How many materials are required to create the project? No more than three separate kinds of products are used for the best Cricut projects: surface content such as a mug or jacket, and something you place on it, including vinyl. Even the super simple ones, including the cardstock for the stacked cards, are nothing more than one sheet.

Techniques: How many techniques are required for the project? The easiest Cricut designs are just one method, such as adding one layer of iron-on-vinyl to a jacket, one layer of adhesive vinyl to a mug, or simply connecting two pieces of cardstock.

Completion Time: How long does it take to complete the project? To beginners, the best Cricut projects are easy to create and take less than two hours in total from start to finish. You will also find quicker items, such as the luminary core or the sweet face mugs. When you have to work so long on a job before you finish it, you can lose concentration or get overwhelmed, and that's not fulfilling. However, should you find any problems — which are common when you're a starter — a shorter job ensures you can easily start again and end?

3.12 Main observations and suggestions

Simple configuration

Don't be scared to dig out the Cricut Maker and launch it! Crafting is a profession for people, and they feel distracted by the beautiful box and all the technology inside items.

Bluetooth

The Bluetooth is embedded in the Cricut Creator and can attach from across the room. Read: This is a lifesaver if you don't have a lot of office space! We had to plug in an old Cricut Explore device into the screen. Most people hack it down on the concrete, literally. You do need to insert the Cricut Creator into an outlet but not your computer. This function allows you to position the system anywhere and break it off from your screen!

Fast mode

This function lets you cut and write 2x more easily! What doesn't want to quickly work on their machine? And it is as easy as clicking on the cut screen on this little icon. People are getting so excited about this function! The quick mode doesn't operate on all products but for vinyl, it's pretty good.

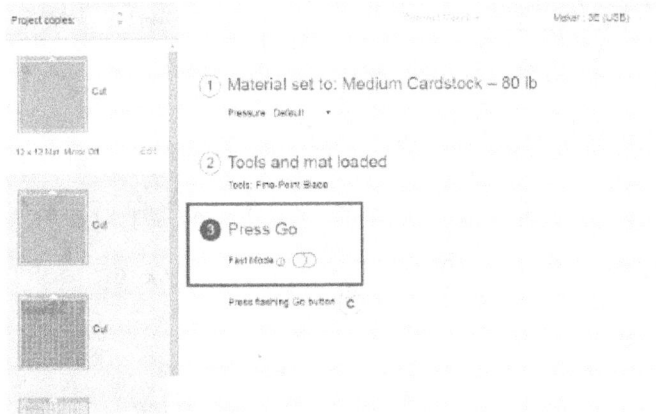

Free ventures in Cricut design space

With any computer, Cricut Design Space has lots of free projects and photos, including gentle baby blocks while you're in the Design Room, left-hand press on the items, then drop down to "Available for Cricut Builder." Also, if you press the "Videos" button on the left and then the "Categories" button at the top of the page, you can find 50 + free photos per week.

Open online SVG-files and designs

Cricut Design Space has a small range of free designs, but you can also search "doc-inset holiday of preference- SVG data" and find more loads online.

The coolest aspect of a device being a developer room is that you can build it wirelessly. For starters, you can cook up a football practice project or pick up a line in the school. You will generate creativity wherever it hits! You can cut the template wirelessly as well when you get home.

Docking &iPhone charging device

The Cricut Creator has a location planned especially for keeping the phone or laptop. Best of all? The unit can be powered too!

Rotary blade

The latest Cricut Creator will cut fabric without the need to install backup! The Cricut Creator was built for cutting cloth.

3.13 Advices:

Pay careful attention to the instructions and can read/watch everything before you proceed. Some of our designs have both instructions written down and a guide so you can pick the path that fits better for you. This should provide detailed guidance on the right Cricut designs on beginners.

For your pre-ready fabrics, equipment, and devices. Our designs often come in a gold box with a list of necessary materials and supplies. Test it and figure out just what a client wants you to do.

Be careful of substitutions. They can succeed, or they can struggle in producing a big art. It's harder to absorb when you're seasoned but when you're a starter that can be a nightmare formula.

Please test first while in doubt! Only cut a little heart out of the corner of a sheet of paper or vinyl to make sure you have the correct settings and pad.

Expect errors. We always commit errors-it's part of the cycle of learning. Allow no anger. Based on how significant the error is, either continue again or just keep going. We all had plenty of goofed up ventures done — now it's all part of their appeal.

Aim for progress over excellence. Your early designs are unlikely to be flawless when it comes to art, even though it is feasible. Be patient with yourself. You are going to be your opponent. If you dispute this, please share a picture of your project in our Cricut Facebook community and ask what others think about it — you'll be shocked by how many see the magic only though you see the errors.

Chapter No. 4 Advanced Cricut Projects with Some Tips

The chapter will provide in-depth information on how you can make advanced projects with the help of this technology and can add creativity to your life.

4.1 Creating Paper Flower Rosettes

One of the cutest and simplest paper flowers to make is the Paper rolled rosettes. These do have other different applications, from bouquets to toppers for gift bags, wreaths, and more. It's no wonder so many of our followers want to learn how to make rosettes from paper!

One rosette's finished scale should be about 3-4 inches. Yet to get more bulk you should still put more than one around!

Materials to Cut & Supplies

- 50-80 lb. cardstock. 65 pounds is what is used in this project here. You can use 8.5 x 11 or 12 x 12size. • Check out the full paper flower supply list here!

- Glue gun

- Wood dowel or quilling tool (optional)

- Fine-point blade

- Standard mat

- Cricut machine (Explore or Maker)

- Rosette templates

Guidelines

If equipped for a cutting tool:

- Download and transfer your SVG cut files to your cutting tools instead.

- Adjust the Display Room Canvas rosette prototype to fill 8.5 x 11 margins or 12 x 12 margins by using 12 x 12 board. When you choose you can still downsize?

- Put your selected document onto the mat.

- Load mat

- Apply the paper to the cardstock. Use medium or hard by weight of paper you've got. Cut start.

If hand cutting.

Paste the design straight onto your cardstock and cut it with scissors afterward. Or print the models onto heavy cardstock once, then draw them with scissors onto your favorite colored cardstock, then cut out the pattern.

4.2 DIY Phone Case with Cricut-How to Design Vinyl Phone Cases

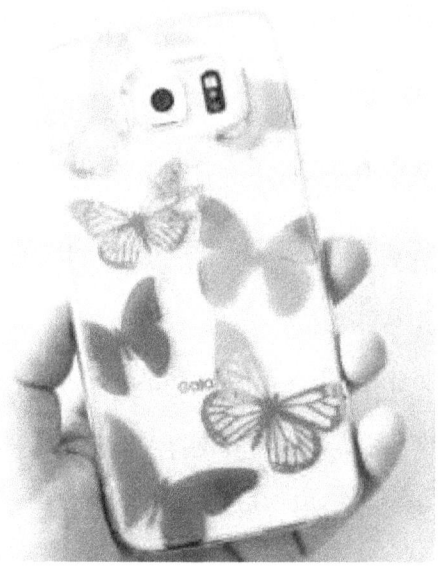

There's an infinite chance of buying a Cricut. Through tiny information such as a phone case to massive designs such as huge paper flowers.

We don't know about you, but it's been a very natural occurrence for everyone to upgrade their phone cover. Purchasing phone cases can be pricey, though, and they rarely offer any customization! Today with the aid of your Cricut and some vinyl teaching you can make a DIY phone cover!

DIY Mobile Case Supplies

- Cricut Maker or Cricut Explore

- Vinyl

- Phone cases

- Weeding tools

- Images or favorite fonts to create designs

- Acrylic sealer

The first step is to load Design Space into your app. Then cut your pic and weed it. Make sure the case size is tested and the picture is scale-up correctly.

Then burn the template onto the tape for delivery. Using Cricut scraper for front and back scraping the vinyl onto the sheet. And take the transfer tape away from the cover.

Group the picture and put it on the camera cover. Use your time with your fingertips or use the Cricut scraper tool to push the picture flat.

Lift your transfer tape carefully, go gradually, and pause if you need to change the record.

It is suggested that sealing the phone case's exterior with mod podge transparent acrylic sealer as a last move. Sealing the material would essentially help keep in place and repel water.

4.3 Supplies for Canvas Art DIY

- Cricut Maker or Cricut Explore

- Iron-on vinyl (heat transfer vinyl)

- Printable vinyl

- Printer

- Regular vinyl

- Transfer tape

- Canvases in preferred size

- Easypress or iron

- Staple remover

- Upholstery stapler

- Scissors

- Watercolor or other clip art of your choice

Find photos for your Canvas work.

The main problem concerning this design project is when and how to create an actual work of art using images. There are 3 ways you can do this.

1. Download the watercolor clipart ready for use like shopping on Freepik and Innovative Site. Aquarelle clipart can also be

sold on Etsy.

2. Using quotations and phrases. If you're more of a person's kind of inspiring art, then type your favorite quotation into Design Space with a beautiful font to display on the canvas.

3. Using this software to turn a specific illustration into a watercolor. You can hit and miss this phase so you should still mess around with it and see what's going on!

When you've picked a picture and submitted it to Design Space, you'll want to resize it to life, suit the layout of your chosen canvas. Please remember, that for the Print Then Cut method, Cricut can only cut a 9.25 x 6.25-inch file. If you are inexperienced with your Cricut computer how to use the Print, Then cut process.

4.4 Layering the canvas template

First things first, the cotton fabric will be separated from the timber frame. You can use a staple remover. DO NOT miss that, because without a smooth surface you won't get a clear binding of the iron-on vinyl to the canvas.

Lay it out on your heat-safe surface until you get the canvas off and cut your HTV down to fit. Place the HTV over the canvas and mount it using your Easypress. For 30 seconds you can adjust Easypress to 330 degrees.

Last, fold the fabric over and staple the wood frame back together. And the final stage is to strip your Print and Cut the image from the printable vinyl and put it in the middle of your canvas lined with vinyl!

4.5 DIY Graduation Cap Gift Box

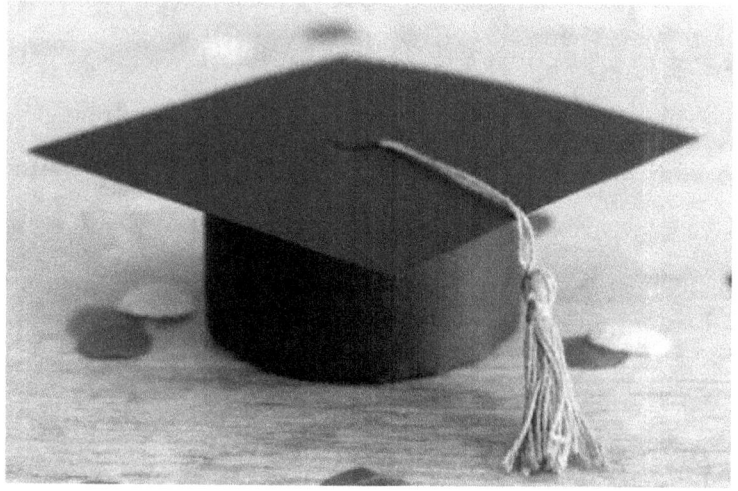

Graduations from this year happen a bit odd. Many are stunned or late, but this doesn't mean they can't be different!

Using a Cricut Creator, Cricut Experiment using SVG software, or your printer with printable PDF files to cut out those grad cap gift boxes.

Below are the materials you would need/want to make your

gift boxes for the graduation pin.

Materials

- Cardstock paper

- Party foil by Cricut

- Gold Brads

- Tombow scrapbooking tape

- Hot glue gun

- Embroidery thread

- Cricut Maker/Cricut Explore or Printer

- Scoring wheel or scoring stylus if using a Cricut machine

You may use scissors to remove the grad cap caps or the Cricut tool. When using the Cricut unit, make sure that you use either the scoring wheel or the scoring stylus, so that the folds are precise.

Using the Template in Design Space

Adjust the black lines on top of the solid template to a scoreline as you put the outline into Design Space, then Add the scoreline to the solid outline.

Printing the Box Template

You can quickly print the PDF file for those who want to cut by hand and follow the directions provided with your freebie to glue and fold the grad cap box.

These gift boxes are a lovely and super enjoyable way to offer money or sweets to a new graduate!

4.6 Minnie Mouse skirts

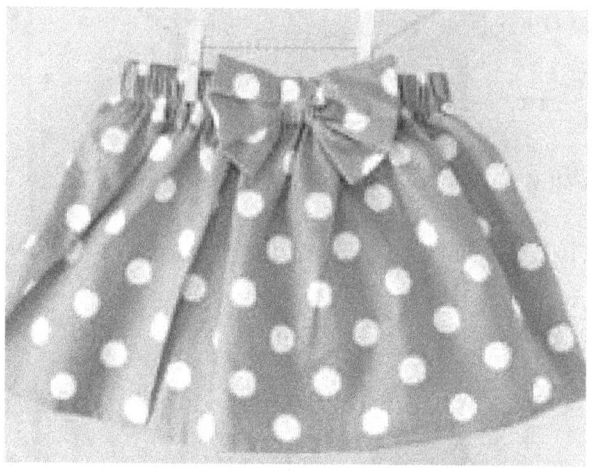

Go for 3 separate Mickey head measurements. Use a 6-inch model for our son, for 4-year-old girl a 5-inch one and a newborn a 4-inch Mickey. Load the heat transfer vinyl into the silhouette cameo and began carving, after had them built and ready to carve.

Replace the extra vinyl after the vinyl was destroyed, so that all that was left on the plastic was Mickey's heads.

Just purchase the Walmart's simple white t-shirts at about $3 each.

Split the heads of Mickey off and put it on the top where needed. When it comes to certain kinds of programs, everyone is not a measurer. Just set it flat and change it to the look you want. Place the plastic shielding sheet at the end. You'll iron on the sheet of plastic. Using the steam from a hot iron and tightly press it down while you hammer over the Mickey handle.

Slowly take off the plastic cover until you have ironed the Mickey flat. If the vinyl edges begin to pop up as you cut the material, then put the material back down and iron it once properly.

You should either keep them as Mickey Mouse or create a bow out of the same cloth that uses for the Minnie Mouse skirts and create a girl's shirts bow.

Use a safety pin, then put the bows right at the top of Mickey's head. And neither do the cute models harm their appeal!

These shirts are genuinely simple and easy to produce. The aspect that took the most on those shirts was for the girl's shirts to create the bows.

4.7 DIY Pastry or Stencil Cake

Draw a circle by the size of the cake's diameter to build flexibility in Design Space.

Build the text you like (feel free to use your ideas). Use the Birthday Bash font, but something that's somewhat blocky can be included. Drag the text and scale it to match inside the rectangle.

You may want to put the lines closer together, depending on the font that you are using. This can be achieved by reducing the line width. You cannot get quite the alignment you like for other fonts yet so there's another easy way to bring the lines together. Select Advanced, then pick Lines Ungroup. That will allow you to push the lines wherever you like.

Pick the whole circle and document, and press Add, until the interface looks the way you like. This will all come together, and it can break off the way you see things on the projector.

To make the cake stencils, give the pattern to your Cricut machine and cut it out on a cardstock or kraft sheet.

You are then ready to decorate this cake!

Using powdered sugar to decorate a dark-colored cake, identical to chocolate. Using chocolate powder to decorate a light-colored egg.

Place the stencil softly over fruit, pastry, or cupcake. Push it down just sufficiently to keep sugar from escaping under the labels, just not so hard to take it up without wrecking the icing.

Load a seaming spoon with powdered sugar or chocolate powder and press the spoon lightly to sift the mixture over the stencil. Completely cover the gaps but seek not to close them too far or you cannot read the letters too.

The sugar is a little thicker than you like on this cupcake but it's always legible. Lift the stencil gently away from the cake to show.

The look is so sweet, and nobody can believe it was so easy!

Create one unique cake or create a couple of different ones and set up a Valentine's Day dessert bar!

4.8 Sleeping Masks for Sewing Beginners

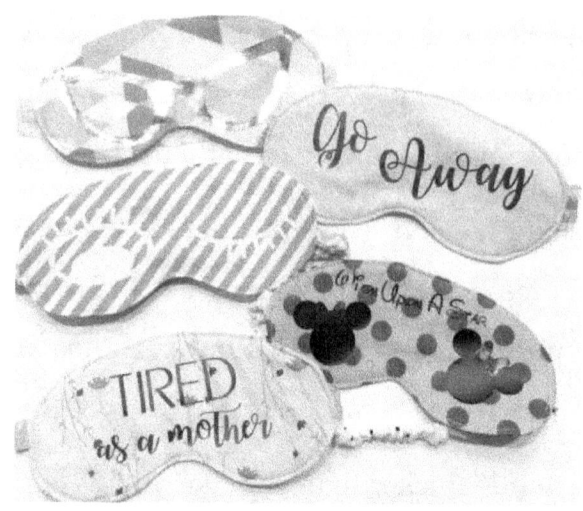

Notice that sewing is not only a simple job but a true pleasure when you know a few essential techniques. So, if you are as motivated as we were, go ahead and try this basic sleeping mask.

Face masks make cool presents, they easily zip together so you can utilize your scraps of cloth. You can personalize them completely and make special them. Let's kick-off!

Supplies:

- 1 to 4 inches X 9 inches Fusible Fleece/cotton batting

- 2 to 5 inches X 9 inches fabric scraps

- 1 to 2 inches X 16 inches fabric scrap for covering elastic –

- This is optional!!

- 1 to 13 inches 1/4 elastic (adults) 11-12 inches elastic (kids) fold over elastic you can use, ruffled premade elastic, or just plain 1/4 inches woven elastic.

Guidelines:

Step 1: Cover the fabric 2 layers and fusible fleece then put the pattern above. Lock, and take it off.

Optional: if an elastic lined cloth is used. Pull the right sides of the fabric together and stitch long edges and leave open the short edges.

You can switch the fabric around to get a section that looks like this. Using instead an elastic safety pin and loop it into the cloth.

Step 2: Put the back fabric on the fusible fleece top facing upwards (so it can be seen easily). Place the cloth with the elastic on. Place the top fabric side-down (you'll see the fabric back) over the others.

Step 3: Pin together your project – or you may use the quilt clips.

Step 4: Together sew the project – leave the gap 1-1.5" and you can transform it straight around.

Step 5: Transform the right side of cloth, iron, and cover the door. Use ladder stitch or the preferred process, you can do stitch together. If you had to add essential oil and rice before closing your door, do so. They're done!

4.9 How to Make Print and Cut Bookmarks

These DIY magnetic bookmarks were simple to use on my Cricut Maker, utilizing the print and cut app. Once the file was imported to my Cricut Design Space save it as a printed and cut document. Place the illustration onto my canvas and resized it to match the scale of the print and the break. (6.75 x 9.25) If you get the project size right, press Print it, and as it is stored as a print and cut paper, submit it directly to your printer.

Type these onto cardstock and then attached my printed page to my cutting pad, with its registration marker. Pick the material as a cardstock, mounted the mat into the system, and struck the computer with the go press. The Cricut detects the entry points and then slashes the bookmarks.

Use a rating device in the center of the bookmarks to score around the dotted lines so they would be simpler to fold. Peel off the magnets' adhesive backrest and add them to thebookmark's inner flaps. Be sure they completely fit before committing to them. Clip it to your book page and they're able to continue maintaining their position.

Using the button below to download the prints and cut DIY magnetic bookmarks. To save the picture to your screen, right-click. Access the file in template space until imported to scale the picture to suit under specifications of print and cut, 6.75 inches long by 9.25 inches in duration. You will need to rotate these 90 degrees and you'll have a decent size portrait model to print and cut.

Cricut cutting machine

If you don't have a Cricut cutting device, you can cut these by hand easily too. You can scale these to the scale you want and only cut them using scissors or a paper cutter.

4.10 DIY Apple Earrings

Upload the cut file named "Apple Earring" into the Layout Room.

The pattern involves a strong earring set and a few colorful bits. You cut a durable replacement and then attach paint with vinyl or paper on top. 2" high are the earrings are, however, you can change the size according to match your look-just be sure you hold it all together!

The pattern is an earring, and you need to create a second one.

Choose the earring template and then press "Duplicate" on the right in the bar of the menu. Tap the "Flip" drop-down button and now "mirror" the picture horizontally of the duplication package chosen. When you choose to make a similar jewelry pendant, you might always replicate the duplication again!

First, you must consider the material you require to create your earrings. There are lots of options luckily, you can use 3 different fabrics using Cricut devices, along with the following supplies:

Along with Cricut Maker:

- Basswood or 2 mm Chipboard

- Knife

- Mat StrongGrip (Purple)

- Brayer

4.10.2 Along with Cricut Explore (can useMaker also):

- Authentic Leather

- StrongGrip Mat (Purple)

- Brayer

- Deep Point Blade

Further Materials:

- Red, green - Glitter Cardstock

- Adhesive

- Red, green - HTV, Iron-On Vinyl

- EasyPress Mat

- EasyPress Mini

- Weeding Tools

- Protective Sheet Iron-On

You prefer to utilize the Cricut Knife to remove chipboard or basswood. The tool is identical to a hobby knife, which helps to accurately hack into harder materials.

You may still require taking some steps before you get going and ensure sure you have a good cut. Next, you need the purple SrongGrip Mat, the stickiest one mat in place for holding hard materials. Put chipboard in the mat top left corner and utilize a brayer to force it as tightly. The Knife cuts in several passes (like using a small knife), and it is suggested that you use it.

Until cutting, make sure to adjust the setting of material to

"Chipboard 2 mm" or "Basswood." The Knife Blade is installed into the unit by removing the Adjustable Clamp B tool system and inserting the blade within, aligning together the gears. To protect the frame, close the clamp.

Since the material becomes heavier, there may be several cutting attempts. Be sure to have a good Bluetooth link, or attach directly to the machine via cord if appropriate. Just be sure your device doesn't "stop" through the cutting phase.

Set to 20 passes at least, so you should stop the cut (don't unload mat) and test the chipboard and see whether it has been sliced through or not.

If the content is sliced, the mat is unloaded and gently extract the sliced template. If you've unloaded the mat for any reason and the template is not entirely cut, use theTrue Control Knife to finish cutting by hand.

Below are the three items cut out for the first attempt. Once cutting fresh products there is also the learning curve. leather earrings cutting are not flawless so here are some valuable tips

- Make sure new is the Deep Point Blade or super clean at least. So rough are the Edges That's why.

- Also, the leather didn't fit in a few cases all through the way, and top layer some parts fell away.

- Place the face-down leather onto the mat for a smoother break!

- Press Very hard the leather, particularly if it is an older pad. For smoother and more uniform pressure use the brayer.

A bit denser basswood is than the balsa wood, and it's great for earrings! When carved, you can leave wood or also apply polish on the top for keeping wood grain. Either you can add color to earrings with some acrylic paint, or the Cricut is used to carve the other half of the design of earrings out of iron-on vinyl or glitter cardstock and put them on the wood top.

- While in comparison to balsa the wood is dense, it's also a little delicate. The good thing is that easily you can put back together, the pieces.

- Press Very hard the wood, particularly if it is an older pad. For smoother and more uniform pressure use the brayer.

Among the 3 products, we believe the most effective was the chipboard! After gently separating mats pieces, use the adhesive to add the pieces of glitter cardstock right on the top. To keep the edges from sticking out, put something on the earring top (like a large book) before the glue sets.

If you'd prefer to utilize vinyl, simply glue the bits on a label and push it down tight with the scraper tool. A further choice is to use the HTV iron-on vinyl Put on the EasyPress Mat, the chipboard, and gently line the iron-on vinyl on the earring top (be sure aligned the holes are).

All you require to do now is install a jumping ring to a hole at the earring top and mount an earring loop to the jumping ring to complete the build!

Hope you will enjoy a nice time creating your apple earrings!

4.11 DIY Hogwarts Set

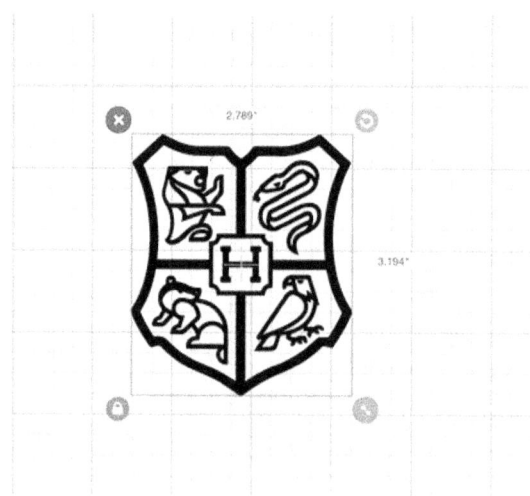

Harry Potter's birthday is coming up and hopes those Harry Potter-inspired crafts ought to be posted! Such coasters at Hogwarts house are the best place to put your goblet when showing off your confidence at Hogwarts. Using this Cricut and a few little tricks, this coaster collection is simple to create for your home décor and will also give fellow Harry Potter fans a fantastic gift idea.

You'll need to continue with these supplies to create these Hogwarts House Coasters:

- Coaster blanks Cricut square

- Infusible Paint Markers in Cricut

- Tape resistant to fire

- Copy paper 3-4 sheets

- Bag plastic Sandwich

- Spray Bottle

- Cricut EasyPress, 9x9

- Cricut EasyPress Mat, 12x12

Using a pencil to draw a coaster gently onto a sheet of copy paper. Place a plastic sandwich bag over the paper and use different shades of red Infusible Ink markers to create spontaneous scribbles. Push the sheet from below, and then gently mist the plastic bag with a water-filled spray bottle.

Place face-down the document softly on top of the bag and click lightly. The ink is quickly transferred to the page, which will provide an impact on the watercolor! When you spray so much mud, you'll see the move look on the wrong leg ... That's not going to work very well, because there's not much ink to infuse!

When you choose to incorporate more color, you can pass more ink for a stunning, layered look of the watercolor and a bolder effect. Just make sure the paper is dry until you add another sheet.

For coaster models, replicate the ink transfer cycle in black, blue, and purple. When the papers are drying and you're pleased with the feel, cut the outlines around 1/4 "bigger than the pencil marks. Be sure the paper is clear, and then you may delete the pencil marks.

Wipe the coaster clean with a lint-free rag. Put the paper face-down on top of the coaster. Tie the edges securely around and keep the edges in place on the back of the coaster with heat-resistant tape.

Place the EasyPress Pad on your desk and put a layer of cardstock to cover your floor. Position the face-down coaster on the cardstock, then put another cardstock sheet on top.

Look to the heat guide to get the exact time and temperature settings for your EasyPress. Position the EasyPress carefully over the coaster and press the green Cricut button to activate the timer.

If the timer beeps, disable the EasyPress carefully. Before attempting to reach or push it, let the coasters cool completely.

Cut the tape and paper to show the coasters until the coasters have cooled off! The paint should be more vivid than the paper and we love how they feel like they've been watercolored!!

Put aside the coasters whilst we are focusing on Harry Potter's next magic move.

Open the Hogwarts Crest SVG (personal usage only) in Design Space. Scale the picture to fit on a 3.5 "x 3.5" coaster. Press the green "Print It" button in the top right corner until you're pleased with the format.

Even for iron-on vinyl, Infusible Ink designs need to be repeated before cutting. Because there are four coasters in this collection, you will need to adjust the number of project copies from 1 to 4 in the drop-down panel. By pressing "Apply," the crests should place on the pad.

You can cut Infusible Ink Transfer Sheets using all the Cricut devices. You'll still need some black Infusible Ink Transfer Sheets, a LightGrip Mat (blue), and tool kit-all designed especially for Cricut Joy use.

Using the weaving equipment to gently extract any pieces of the design that don't fit. Since you may inadvertently leave marks or lose any of the Infusible Ink by scratching the fabrics, We are trying to clean the exterior layer while weeding away the inner portion of the design. It takes fingertips off the design because every tincture that rubbed off is from a component that can be discarded after it is extracted.

Wipe the coasters clean with a lint-free rag. Face-down on the coaster, put the Infusible Ink transfer sheet, and force it down tightly. When appropriate, keep it in position with heat-resistant tape.

Position the EasyPress Pad on your desk and put a sheet of cardstock to cover the pad. Put the coaster face-up on the cardstock this time and position a strip of butcher paper on top. Position the EasyPress softly on the coaster and press the green Cricut button to start the timer.

When the timer beeps, disconnect the EasyPress cautiously. Without trying to reach or push it, let the coasters cool COMPLETELY!! They'll be hot!

Clear the Infusible Ink sheets from your coasters. Use tweezers to extract tiny parts if appropriate. Do not use steel wool, colored cleaning agents, or scrubbing pads to make the coasters look their finest!

4.12 Treat Boxes Valentine's Day

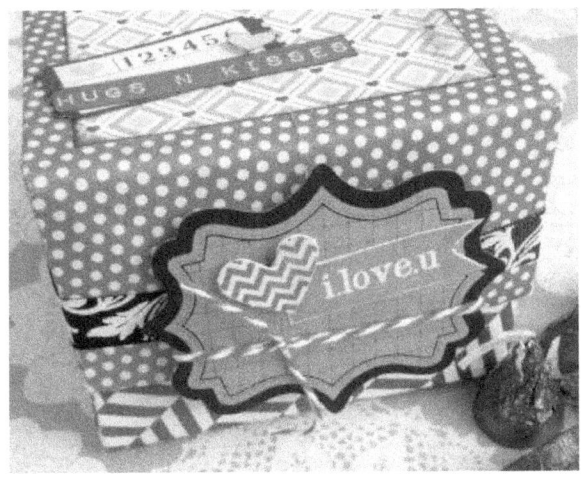

Valentine's Day activities are so much fun to do. If you want cookies or other surprises, these Valentine's Day Gift Boxes are so simple and enjoyable to create for those you love!

You'll need below things to create these cute treat boxes:

- Cricut machine or Cricut Maker

- Valentine's Day Box cut file

- 12 "x 12" Cricut Soft Grip Pad

- Cricut Cardstock: Stylus WhiteCricut scoring

- Pens Cricut: wood, jade, sparkling blue

- Double Tape

Open the Valentine's Day Treat Box in Design Space and change the pen colors, paper colors, and most notably CUT the template of the package out!

One thing to appreciate about the Cricut Maker is how simple it is to use it. It takes you through the method from the beginning to the end. From picking the material to cutting, the device can let you know when to change tools or alert you to put the cap on.

Once the cut is done, extract the box template from the mat wisely. To avoid curling of the pad, transform the mat face down and then slice away the mat from the surface. The mat should fold away from the pad (instead of the opposite), leaving the box template smooth and strong!

To cover the heart cutout on the front of the package, cut a strip of transparent cellophane. The cellophane would encourage you to see the candy through the cutout, without the candy dropping out!

Flip the prototype box over and place a few double-sided tape lines to all sides of the heart. Put the sheet of cellophane right over the head.

Turn the box around and spread gently down both score lines. Apply double-sided tape to the tab on the left side of the case.

Bring all sides together and place the tab under the other edge.

Drop in the tabs at the bottom to cover the package. Begin from the biggest "U" shaped tab and drop at the ends of the side tabs. Finally, fold at the end of the last tab and the bottom of the package should remain locked. The box is remarkably durable so you should put a strip of tape around the edges if you're concerned about it breaking open.

Fill the box with your favorite Valentine treats. Put both handles together to cover the package and stick the tabs in the sides of the box with the "keyhole."

What a "special" present for friends, relatives, or even Valentine's Day instructor! For a nice surprise, you can write a little note or even put a gift card in the package. You can send the package a touch of a new feel by adjusting the pen colors.

4.13 Tips

Let us guide you into the world of Cricut before turning your device on and beginning your very first job. Many wishes somebody had explained such stuff to them before starting on the first design, and this book can lead you.

Your Structure in The Kitchen Is About to Get Pinterest Worthy.

You remember all the cool bottle labels that you've been

pinning. And however, you want, you will configure them. Yet surprise warning, if any people see what you've done in your house, you better assume they're going to invite you to come over and mark theirs too. Let the Cricut Parties start!

The printing of labels for plain pantry bins, refrigerator drawer labels, and these Spice Jar labels are some perfect novice ideas for kitchen organization.

You May Need a Designated Room

The Maker is a piece of chunky machinery so you would require a decent room to use it. Now is the time to cut out a guest bedroom area or the odd nook in your dining room that you have never understood what to do with before. It's certainly worth having all your creative things in one usable place, even if it's only a little closet.

If you are ready to start configuring space for your craft here's the Must-Have List:

A table, sofa, or countertop, and a convenient chair. Extra points whether they have spokes on the chair.

• Space for storage. This device is not super powerful, but it is not light either, so don't expect to put it on a shelf that is very big or short. My preferred place to put it is on this moving cart, but with little effort, you can hold it somewhere it is easy to get to.

• Good illumination. It is so crucial because you can know that you need the finest pair of glasses and ultra-bright lighting after you see the video lessons and learn more about weeding. The overhead light should not interrupt the ceiling fan. Move into the office for LED job illumination.

• Storage containers. You might have begun by buying a package, or you might only purchase proceeds on a project-by-project basis. Whatever path you take, you'll end up selling a ton of stuff. Use transparent lidded containers to divide your equipment and materials, and make sure you use your latest Maker to mark your containers and keep it clean and smooth.

You 're Going to Want Components

Besides the Builder, Cricut has plenty of cool attachments that will make your projects look much better, quicker, simpler, and more professional.

The BrightPad is an utter favorite add-on tool. It's essentially liked a tablet-shaped lightbox that artists use to draw, so while you're making delicate cuts it makes weeding SO much simpler.The Vital Pack, the Compact Trimmer, and the Extra

Wide Self-Healing Cutting Pad are all widely recommended for grabs. In a single project using these bad boys. Take it from the kid who can't cut a straight line to save her life, so any scissor break is jagged like a bread knife. If you've been raised with a sharp edge in one side so tweezers in the other, place some tool kits on your Mother's Day Wishlist.

Extra Cutting Mats Are Required.

Maybe not instantly but intend to get some extra mats in the span of a few months after you got confident with the unit. When you continue to venture into advanced designs, you may need to print on various shades and fabrics on separate sheets, so you can save a lot of energy from not needing to stop the printing when you are peeling vinyl off the cutting mat so that you can use it again.

Suggest 3-4 regular mats and 2 or three of the solid yet fragile grip mats. You can fill them all up by holding extra on hand until you press send, and then roll on in.

Initially opt for Removable Vinyl

This needs a little bit of time to get accustomed to working with vinyl as a novice. You're going to make missteps; you're going to misplace it and you're going to break a bunch of sheets. `Starting with clear vinyl helps you to get your feet wet without daily effort.

When you've perfected the removable vinyl designs, you'll bring your big girl socks on and start stamping your universe forever.

The Creator Does More Than Just Score and Cut.

One of the favorite Cricut Maker apps is that it can compose just the same as it cuts with markers. That means if you don't have such fantastic handwriting but still want to create a personalized Mother's Day card, you can still pull the cool handwritten font off without even taking a Scripting lesson.

Cricut offers a large range of fun pens and markers and all you need to do is drop them into the pen holder, set up the template in Design Space and label it as Draw instead of Cut. Within minutes, you have a professional-looking typewritten font for whatever project you like. We love to use the Special Card Draw app, party invites, place cards, school projects, and binder covers.

Design Space has Licensed Brands!

It is such an amazing incentive for any of the efforts to come. Aside from all the fun models and premade designs available in Design Space, the favorite characters of your children may even be cut or illustrated. From Star Wars and Marvel and Disney, and much more, with their beloved TV BFFs, you will deck out your kid's clothing, bedrooms, and school supplies.

The Kids May Continue to Make as Much Use of It as You Do.

Since the moment you unboxed Cricut Builder, your kid will always think of all the fun he'll do with it. View the instructional videos, hear, and brainstorm everything a vinyl label could hold on. The Maker encouraged children to settle in an imaginative mind and build different stuff they can do.

When you have older children then make them know how to use the Creator while you do so, and you all stay encouraged and excited to use your latest investment, and don't let it scare you. The printing of iron-on for clothes and backpacks, bedroom storage stickers, binder covers, and paper-crafting projects are some excellent beginning ideas for youngsters. You will find many of these already built for you in the Project Room.

The First Project Can Fail.

Bring this in last because everybody is being pressured. You have opened the package, seen the photos, purchased the products, and you are exhausted now. Because the original concept can fail. People were having too much fun. They have not thought that was a waste of resources. We didn't sound like they were losing time down there. We taught how to prevent weeding, filing, and transfer. And in their second attempt, they are through.

The greatest thing you can consider, and the main lesson, is that your Cricut Creator isn't just a machine. This is an event. There is likely to be a lot of trial and error. Hiccups can be there. And there may be occasions that you dump the whole idea to get going again. So, if you start low, and work your way up, you're going to be surprised at the stuff you can make.

Conclusion

Cricut is a revolutionary cutting tool which offers you an easy way to cut the designs you need. It is not only simple and effective but one of the top Cricut products and some would argue that it is the best on the market.

A great guide is this book for new beginners in the Cricut world. You should learn the fundamentals of the machine using, the different types of devices, which one fits you, and how the Cricut device is set up. A complete chapter is devoted to the crafts for the beginners that will help the beginners to understand how to utilize the grip mats, the materials, and what sort of settings should be utilized to produce the sort of outcome wanted by you. Similarly, advanced designs are also in it along with tips and advice. You can utilize the device for projects of all sorts like home decor, party decoration, wedding signs, toys, handmade cards, and much more.

We hope this Cricut for Beginners can help you begin to learn how to create a basic project and get over the new feeling in Cricut.

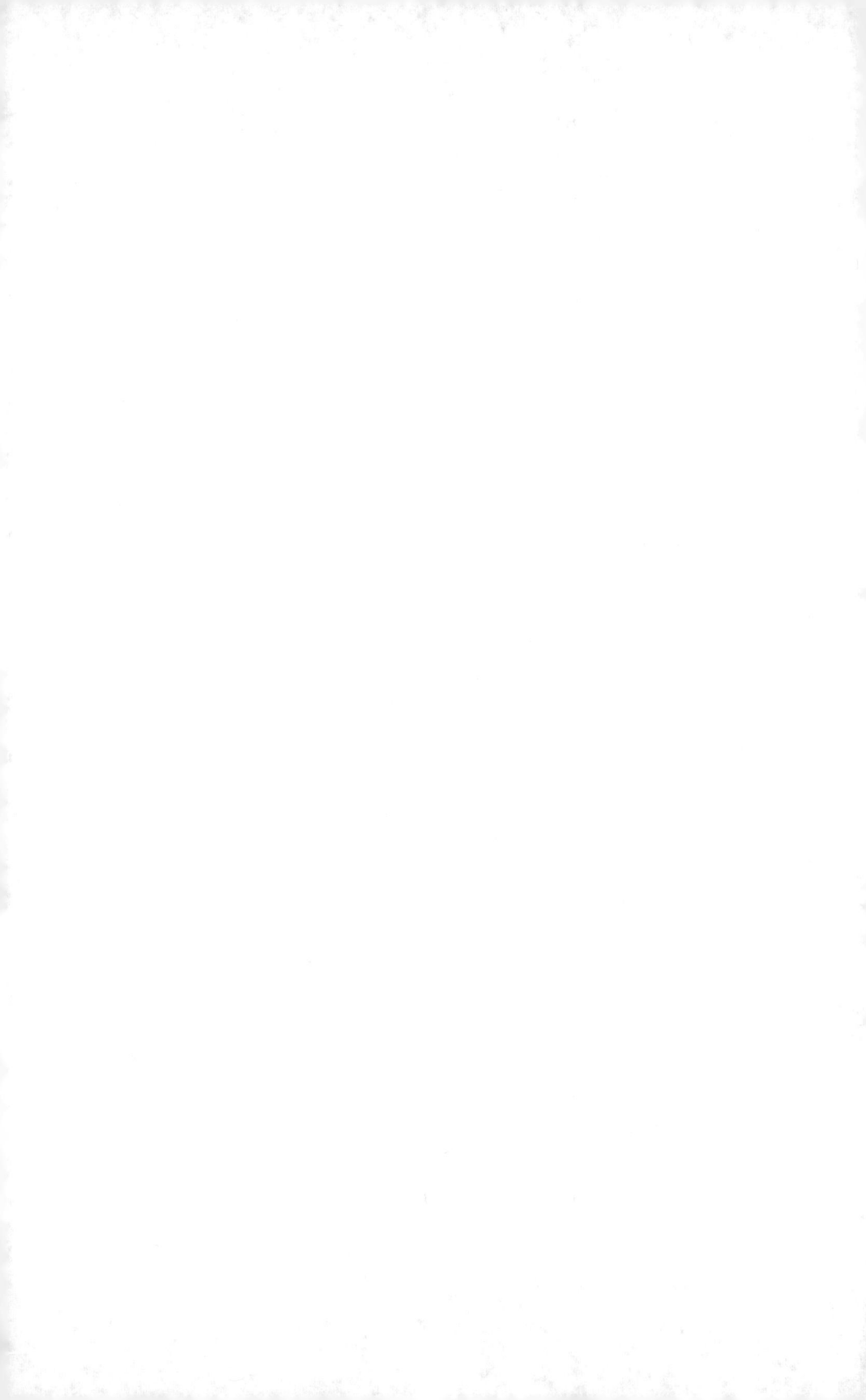

www.ingramcontent.com/pod-product-compliance
Lightning Source LLC
Chambersburg PA
CBHW070354220526
45467CB00001B/381